COPING WITH STRESS AT WORK

Jacqueline M. Atkinson

Thorsons
An Imprint of HarperCollins*Publishers*

Thorsons
An Imprint of HarperCollins*Publishers*
77–85 Fulham Palace Road,
Hammersmith, London W6 8JB

Published by Thorsons 1988
5 7 9 10 8 6 4

© Jacqueline M. Atkinson 1988

Jacqueline M. Atkinson asserts the moral right to
be identified as the author of this work

A CIP catalogue record for this book
is available from the British Library

ISBN 0-7225-1485-9

Printed in Great Britain

COPING WITH STRESS AT WORK

Contents

Introduction

Stress—the very word can conjure up symptoms of itself. Muscles tighten. Heart rate increases. Breathing seems more rapid and shallower. Is this what we mean by stress? In part, yes. But what about that sense of panic when we realize we have too much to do and not enough time in which to do it? Or the feeling we experience when we get home from work and cannot wait to have a drink, then snap at our family, or collapse in front of the television, too tired and apathetic to do anything else? All these reactions might be manifestations of stress.

Both the person who is too lethargic to do anything and the person who *always* has to do something may be experiencing stress. 'Don't know the meaning of the word', says the young executive, cigarette clenched between his teeth, skin pallid and muscles flabby as he thrusts his way, elbows out, up the next rung of the ladder. A similar man or woman might be heard to mutter, 'Stress? Couldn't do without it. It's what pushes me on.'

We might be stressed and not know it, or at least refuse to acknowledge it. We might even see it as positive—something that motivates us. How many people do you know who say they work better to a deadline— the shorter the better? How often have you done something at the last minute, in a rush and a panic, that could have been done before at a more leisurely pace? Or maybe you have complained to others about how busy you are, how rushed, how little sleep you are getting, to impress upon them, and maybe yourself too, that you *are* a busy person and also, by implication, hard-working, conscientious and important? Unfortunately, the result may be that people see you simply as inefficient.

Stress comes at us from all sides and hits us in different ways. We have to learn to deal with it, eliminating it where possible and desirable, in other cases coping with it as best we can and even, on occasion, using it in a positive way.

Before we can begin coping we have to learn where stress comes from and what causes it in our life. We also need to discover if we actually *are* stressed and, if so, what effect this is having on us. Over the course of reading this book I hope that one of the things that will become clear to you is that it is your attitude to things that happen to you, and even to stress itself, which causes part of the problem.

All of us have our own ways and patterns of coping with stress and potential stressors. Sitting and feeling sorry for yourself and berating 'them' is as much a way of dealing with stress as reaching for the whisky bottle or a cigarette 'to calm your nerves'. But are these really the best ways of dealing with stress and tension? What alternatives are there? Most people think first of some form of relaxation to ease the tension out of the body or some form of exercise to release it in a burst of energy and thus 'work it out of the system'. Both can be useful but is this all there is to coping?

For most of us the answer is no. Relaxation and exercise can form part of stress management but rarely are they the whole answer as they do not deal with what causes you to become tense in the first place. Let us look at an example.

You are in a meeting and no one is taking your point of view seriously. You start to feel angry, resentful, frustrated or depressed. Good relaxation skills may stop you tensing your muscles, feeling stressed, developing a headache, or whatever, so that you leave the meeting relaxed; you have 'coped' with stress, but have you solved your problem?

Clearly the answer is no, because you still have not put your point across. This may be because your communication skills are poor and you do not explain clearly. Perhaps pressure of time prevented you from doing your homework properly and so you are unaware of new developments. Or maybe the others can see you have not thought things through and they do not want to take the time to explain where you went wrong. You may believe, deep down, that you do not really merit listening to and so you put on a very unconvincing show or let others talk you down. You need both to find out where your problem lies—whether with your behaviour or attitude or a combination of both—and then to develop the appropriate skills to overcome it. If you always give in to others you will end up feeling like a doormat. If you practise relaxation you may end up a relaxed doormat rather than a tense one but everybody will continue to walk all over you. And now you are not showing signs of stress or tension, they will walk over you with an easier conscience.

Thus the approach taken in this book centres around the two complementary issues of attitude and skill. Examining and challenging your beliefs and developing new ways of thinking are just as valuable skills as learning how to manage your time more efficiently. Although we concentrate on stress in the work environment, the techniques you learn, first in analysing what is causing stress and then in managing it, can be applied to all areas of your life.

The emphasis is on recognizing stress and taking responsibility for it, but this is appropriate only up to a point. All the skills in the world will not protect you, or help you manage completely, in a society or organization which promotes and encourages stress through its attitude, expectations, and basic philosophy to work and personal relationships. You cannot expect to change generations of ideas and traditions or heavily marketed images on your own. If you are serious about managing stress these wider issues need to be faced. The individual cannot resolve them, but if you work collectively, politically, change will occur.

One last word on using this book. As we have stated, it sets out to teach you how to analyse what is causing the stress in your life and then how to develop the skills needed to combat such stress. But reading is not enough. You have to work to learn these skills and then put them into practice. This involves motivation, commitment and patience. It has taken you some time, years maybe, to get where you are today —stress included—and you cannot expect everything to change overnight. In life, there are no magic formulas.

I
Is stress a problem?

1
Are you stressed?

Most people would assume that they know the answer to this question without needing to think about it—a clear 'yes' or 'no'. But is it really that easy? Could you possibly be stressed and not know it? These are some of the issues we must consider first.

Some people who lead busy, active lives, rushing from one thing to another, never seem to experience stress. They see every new task as a challenge to be fitted into their busy schedule. They are the sort of people who leave the rest of us panting in their wake, wondering how they manage to do so much and not collapse under the strain.

Then we know other people who lead relatively quiet, uneventful lives, without much to do and plenty of time in which to do it, and yet who are weighed down by the cares of the world, harried and stressed, and clearly not enjoying their lot. Why should there be this difference?

It is not just a case of a particular task, situation, personality, attitude, or habit causing the problem single-handed, but a subtle combination of all these, and more. The same situation can cause people to experience stress in a wide variety of ways.

Imagine you have to cross town, during the busy lunch-time period, and time is important. You *have* to be there promptly. How do you set about this? How do you react? Maybe you decide to drive yourself there. You know the journey should take 20 minutes but now here you are sitting in a slow-moving line of traffic. How do you respond?

You may feel angry, particularly at the people in the cars in front of you; what right have they to be out now? Couldn't they have travelled at a different time? And as for the idiot who is causing the hold-up—words fail you. Even if there is no one person causing the problem, but say a burst water-main causing a diversion, you blame God, the universe or at least the water board for doing this to *you*, now, when you are in such a hurry. You may find yourself shifting in your seat, straining forward as though that will help you move faster, clenching your muscles, particularly jaw and fists (the latter might descend on the horn periodically), your shoulders and neck tense and your shoulders creep up around your ears. You might light a cigarette (or chain-smoke several), clenching it between your teeth. As you become more and more tense your foot pushes down on the accelerator and you knock bumpers with the car in front. Throughout you maintain your aggressive thoughts towards others.

Maybe you start out feeling angry but, unlike the first person, you turn this anger on yourself. 'Why does this always happen to me?' you accuse yourself, as you remember being caught in similar situations in the past. If there is more than one line of traffic you might start berating yourself for joining the 'wrong' one, as the other lane begins to move and your's doesn't. You begin to question your judgement. As you become more annoyed at yourself you find your shoulders drooping, your whole body slumping, your face taking on a sad expression as you feel more and more inadequate, useless and a failure.

Maybe panic, not anger, is your initial reaction. The traffic hold-up means the journey will take more time than you have. And you *must* be there promptly. As you keep looking at your watch you notice that your breathing has speeded up a bit, it feels as though your heart has palpitations, your stomach turns over and churns, your hands become clammy and sweat breaks out on your forehead and upper lip. You squirm in your seat, shifting so much that your foot falls off the pedal and you stall the car. Your main thought is 'What shall I do?' You can stay in the traffic, knowing that you will be late, and maybe blow the deal, or you can try to find a phone, explain that you will be late, and consequently be even later. Both indecision and panic mount as you keep repeating 'What shall I do?'

Yet again, you might have an initial response of either anger or panic, but quickly realize there is nothing to be done. You are trapped in the slow-moving traffic and that's that. This realization forces you consciously to come to terms with the situation, take several deep breaths and wriggle your shoulders to release tension and turn your thoughts to more pleasant and rewarding topics. You switch the radio on to listen to music, or play your favourite cassette. You may decide to use the time profitably, by running through the points of the meeting again or listening to the news.

Are you one of those people who are having trouble in thinking themselves into the scenario? You want to change the details immediately? Maybe you would not have put yourself in this position in the first place. You know that lunch-time traffic is slow in your part of town, so you would have left more time—therefore there would be no need for panic or agitation.

Of course, the really organized and stress-free will have arranged for a taxi to pick them up in plenty of time, so they are free from the stress of driving themselves as well as from time pressures, and can sit back, relax and settle into the most positive frame of mind for the meeting.

There are always variations. Your only response might have been, 'They should be coming to me.'

There is one last group—those of you who are sitting in the car, knowing you will be late but not caring, convinced that the other person will wait for you and that you will be able to talk your way out of it, with a brief smile, a wave of the hand, and a 'sorry—traffic!' More than likely you are dictating work into a tape recorder throughout the journey, and enjoying the rush, the pushing, the 'just making it', and the physiological changes and feelings that go with this.

Which of these sketches comes closest to describing your reaction in this situation? Your response may vary sometimes, depending on your mood or on what else is going on in your life, but overall your response to this and similar scenarios will be consistent. Although this example is of a short-term stressor, your pattern of responding to all sorts of stresses, both short and long-term, will be similar.

Chronic tension may result from anger, be it directed at others or at yourself, if that anger does not find some satisfactory form of release. And even if it does, anger is not necessarily the most useful or acceptable reaction to such events. Feelings of panic may lead to a person feeling anxious most of the time, with all the unpleasant symptoms this implies.

To deal with either tension or anxiety you may find yourself reaching for a calming cigarette, a comforting bar of chocolate, or a fortifying drink. You may try to work harder and longer, believing that if you could only get up to date/spend an extra hour at the office/do that bit *more*, then your problems would be solved. So you turn into a 'workaholic', see less of your family, have no leisure, and *still* find you are stressed.

Another approach would be to release tension or anxiety in a different situation over which you feel you have more control. So you may pick a fight with your spouse, nag the kids, snap at the barman/ticket collector/neighbour and be generally unpleasant to all around you. Such behaviour will, in turn, lead to further problems and stresses. (Of course, there are adaptive ways of releasing tension and anxiety which we will discuss in chapter 7.) You will then find yourself caught in a vicious spiral as stress leads to problem behaviour which leads to more stress and difficulty in coping. It is important to see the situation as a spiral and not a circle—things become progressively worse, they *do not* stay the same. You are on your way down, heading towards major problems.

This means looking at how you behave and how you think to establish whether you are stressed or not. Stress does not affect everyone in the same way, as we have seen, and even symptoms in the same general area may show themselves in different ways. For example, one person may lose his appetite and not want to eat much at all, whereas another will find herself eating more, whether she is hungry or not. Lots of people will say they have sleep problems, but very different ones. It might be that you have difficulty falling asleep in the first place, or that you wake up in the wee small hours and cannot get back to sleep. Then again, you may be sleeping longer than usual—and still not feeling rested. Getting out of bed may be the first and biggest hurdle of the day.

Symptoms of stress vary from person to person, for many reasons which we will discuss later, but in part they may be associated with other conditions, which influence how signs and symptoms develop and are presented. Before we come to measure stress we must consider the major types of 'stress styles' and related behaviour.

STRESS STYLES AND RELATED PROBLEMS

The hard-driving style

The 'hard-driving style' or 'overdrive' is related to the concept of the Type A personality (which will be considered in detail in chapter 4—see pages 45-57). It means living fast, doing everything quickly, getting upset, frustrated and angry at delays, incompetence and 'acts of God'; it means being highly competitive, wanting to do better and better, beating not just yourself, but others too, excelling, coming first all the time, winning and not settling for second place. It means being completely achievement-orientated—always.

This is a difficult lifestyle to assess, because it can both *lead* to stress and be a *response* to stress. It can also be a lifestyle for high achievers who say they are not stressed and who, by most criteria do not appear stressed. All too many of us believe (or desperately *want* to believe) we fall into this category, that stress truly does not affect us, but all the time, this lifestyle is insidiously taking its toll. The next chapter looks at how build-up of stress affects our health, and how we can misread signs, believing that stress has vanished, when we are simply in another stage of the process.

We have all read about, or seen interviews with, some of the leaders of industry and commerce who rise in the early hours of the morning, are in the office by 7 a.m., stay there until 10 p.m. or 11 p.m., and seem to thrive on it. What we do not see are those who tried this and dropped dead in their forties or fifties; who burnt out and are shells of their former selves; or who keep going, not very successfully, on an unstable combination of drink, drugs, anxiety and willpower.

Those who manage, survive and even enjoy this hard-driving lifestyle *and* reach the top are, almost by definition, exceptional. To take such people as role models for ourselves is, in most cases, a mistake. Most of us need to lead more balanced lives to be healthy and happy.

It is all too easy to convince ourselves that we *can* cope, that we enjoy this way of living and that it does us no harm. Research in this area is somewhat equivocal, but just because you can think of one, or even 10 people who live like this, and have not (yet) had a coronary, that does not mean that it is acceptable for us all to live like this. We all know someone who smoked 60 cigarettes a day all his life and died in healthy old age when knocked down by a car! Just because one person avoids lung cancer does not mean that you would advocate cigarette smoking as part of a healthy lifestyle, does it?

Anxiety

It is quite possible to be anxious and not be stressed, or stressed and not anxious, although the latter may be less common. Many of the signs of anxiety are similar to early signs of stress (see chapter 2). Anxiety might be part of the reason you are stressed, or be a response to stress.

Anxiety, like stress, can be a transitory state, a phase you pass through, or it can be a more chronic, pervasive way of life, and is usually seen as a personality trait (see chapter 4).

In the first case you can worry or be anxious about something specific—you are going to ask your boss for a rise, you have an important presentation to make, or you are going for an interview. These are things that make everyone anxious, and are to some extent realistic, but your anxiety may get out of hand, particularly if it is linked to unrealistic ideas (which will be discussed later—see pages 37-9). Where anxiety is realistic it can be useful in stopping us from progressing too soon or too far, or in showing us what we need to learn before we carry on. Anxiety *should* be protective—it becomes a problem only when it stops us doing what we want to do. Not all anxieties are rational, even when they are linked to something specific—you might be anxious about lifts, travelling by plane, or speaking in public. In their more extreme form these fears are known as phobias. They can be extremely crippling and are outside the scope of this book; they may require professional therapy to deal with them. (Ask your GP for a referral to a clinical psychologist.)

Sometimes the anxiety may not be linked to anything in particular but just be 'a mood you are in'; this often means anxiety is a personality trait.

As well as the physiological signs—everything from palpitations, sweating and shallow breathing to feeling faint, trembling or tension—anxiety will be accompanied by feelings of fear, worry or dread.

Helplessness and hopelessness

Martin Seligman, an American psychiatrist, has described a clinical condition of helplessness and its relationship to depression. For some people it may also be a response to stress. You feel helpless, in the face of overwhelming odds, to do anything about the stress you are experiencing: helpless to change yourself, to change others, to change your physical situation or the demands being made on you. A sense of hopelessness sweeps over you when you consider the future. You may become apathetic, doing what you have to do and no more; you give up searching for solutions to the problem and, usually, you also give up trying to avoid the problem or situation. You take whatever comes at you with little or no response. In a milder form this helplessness may take the pattern of mentally opting out, fantasizing about other things altogether, or looking back to how things used to be. But in the present the person sees no options, no way of changing things and, most importantly, no way out in the future.

Depression

I mention depression here because it can be confused with stress but, although it may be a response to some types of stress, it is generally a very different problem. Some of the symptoms might be the same but not all. Depression is sometimes considered to mean feeling sad, unhappy or 'down', but clinical depression involves other symptoms, such as withdrawal, slowed thinking and moving, agitation, problems with concentration, feelings of guilt, self-reproach and self-depreciation.

Insomnia is usual, eating patterns are disrupted and loss of libido is common.

If you suspect that you are (or someone else is) depressed rather than stressed then you should consult a doctor. Depression can arise for many reasons, some of them biochemical, and all avenues should be explored, in terms of causes and treatment.

Burnout

Burnout is an extreme reaction to a continuing stressful situation. Although there has been some description of, and research into, executive burnout, the term tends to be used in relation to the caring professions. Nurses and social workers figure prominently in the research but also involved are teachers, doctors, dentists and clergy. Increasingly the term is applied to people succumbing to stress in a variety of people-orientated service industries.

Symptoms of burnout include apathy, helplessness and hopelessness, overlaid with cynicism and possibly selfishness. Most people who suffer burnout work as part of a bureaucratic organization, often state-run, probably under-funded and usually subject to cuts; they may have low pay and/or status, work in isolation with little social support, have reached career plateaux with little chance of advancement and, most importantly, be faced with demanding clients and no clear criteria of success or even task completion (for example, where one client/patient is immediately replaced by another, and there is known to be a long waiting list).

The most common response to burnout is to leave both the job and the profession. Bitterness may pervade the individual who then has difficulty settling in any job. Burnout is an extreme and severe response which probably requires professional intervention.

THE POSITIVE ASPECTS OF STRESS

Not all stress is seen as negative. We have already mentioned the people who seem to thrive on a fast-paced, hard-driving lifestyle that would leave most of us exhausted. What is happening to those people who actively seem to court stress?

Such people are rarely aware of the potential stress in a situation. What some of us might describe as a demand or threat they will see as a challenge or an exciting risk. This means that each new task is positive rather than negative. The risks these individuals take in their craving for excitement may border at times on the foolhardy, but they get a positive emotional charge or 'high' from the experience. The reasons for this elation are tied to the physiology of stress; essentially these people are addicted to their own noradrenalin, the chemical produced in response to stress. In this way 'stress', now redefined as 'each new challenge', motivates a person to further achievement.

A number of factors we will be considering throughout the book may influence whether something is seen as a negative demand or a positive change. Personality and attitude clearly play a part, but so do factors intrinsic to the task, particularly the amount of control you have over it.

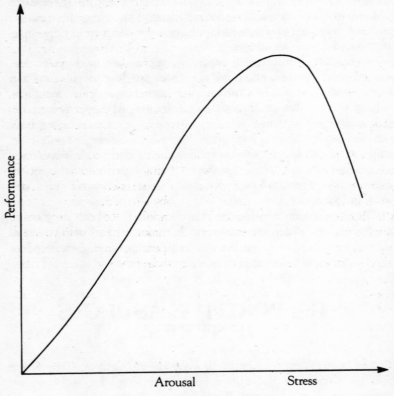

Fig 1   The arousal curve

We cannot get rid of all stress and neither should we try. It can act both as an early warning signal that something is wrong and we must protect ourselves, as well as being a motivator to push us on to bigger and better things. The secret is knowing that there is a balance between too much and too little stress, or to use a more appropriate word, arousal. Knowing your tolerance levels means you are well on the way to winning the war against stress.

The so-called 'arousal curve' (see Fig 1) is well known but worth considering again. The arousal axis is sometimes called anxiety. As can be seen from the diagram, a certain amount of 'arousal', 'anxiety', 'stress'—call it what you will—is needed to motivate the individual to do anything at all—the 'performance' axis.

With no arousal, for example when we are asleep, we have no performance; as arousal increases so does performance. Thus arousal improves performance, but only up to a point.

There comes a time when arousal begins to interfere with performance, which then begins to trail off. To add more arousal at this point in the form of increased pressure will only cause performance to decline further. We all have to learn how much 'stress' we need to get us going—and how much is 'too much' and defeats its object. For example, many of us say we work better to a deadline—it gets us going and keeps us going. But to be useful it has to be realistic. You have to be able to do the work in the required time. The appropriate use of deadlines will be considered along with other ways of managing your time in chapter 9.

From the arousal curve it becomes clear that too little 'stress' can be as much of a problem as too much. Being bored and fed-up with your job does not necessarily mean you are stressed—you may have an exciting social life or a challenging hobby which makes up for your job—but it is worth considering as a component of your problem if you feel under-used and that you are not making the most of yourself. If you are in a job that has occasional slack periods, especially if it follows a busy time (for example, after the rush of work at the end of the financial year), you may find the time drags rather than finding it relaxing. Paradoxically, the less you have to do the more you may resent the work that does come your way: it is not enough to push you up the curve into optimal performance.

CHECKING YOUR STRESS LEVEL

The checklists given in this book to help you assess your stress levels and potential to become stressed are not designed as questionnaires from which to obtain a score, but rather as lists of symptoms, behaviours or problem areas for you to check out in yourself. In many cases it is important to note not just *whether* the behaviour occurs, but whether there has been a *change* in your behaviour. Change is more likely to indicate recent stress or that some new, possibly small, stressor, has been added to an already long-term stress problem.

It should go without saying that the checklists should be answered as honestly as possible, but it is as well to be aware that most of us try to present as good a picture of ourselves as we can when filling in this type of questionnaire—even if the only person who sees it is us.

For Checklist 1, the more behaviours you answer 'sometimes' or 'often' to, the more likely you are to be suffering from stress. If you answer 'never' to more than a few questions check that you are not trying to present too positive a picture of yourself.

You may feel some of the questions do not represent a change in your behaviour, but describe the way you usually behave, for example, 'talk fast' or 'walk fast'. You may feel, therefore, that these should not count in a stress score. Before you dismiss them read chapter 4 on the Type A personality (see page 47).

There are, in addition, two questions which require a yes/no response.

	Yes	No
● Is your mood fixed, and different from usual? (i.e. Are you unusually elated or depressed?)	☐	☐
● Have your daily habits changed suddenly? (i.e. Have you suddenly become very disorganized or highly methodical?)	☐	☐

Checklist 1 Behavioural signs of stress

How often do you:	Often	Sometimes	Rarely	Never
● Feel irritable?	☐	☐	☐	☐
● Feel restless?	☐	☐	☐	☐
● Feel frustrated at having to wait for something?	☐	☐	☐	☐
● Talk fast?	☐	☐	☐	☐
● Walk fast?	☐	☐	☐	☐
● Slump?	☐	☐	☐	☐
● Drag your feet when you walk?	☐	☐	☐	☐
● Become easily confused?	☐	☐	☐	☐

	Often	Sometimes	Rarely	Never
• Have memory problems?	☐	☐	☐	☐
• Think about negative things all the time?	☐	☐	☐	☐
• Think about negative things without wanting to?	☐	☐	☐	☐
• Have marked mood swings?	☐	☐	☐	☐
• Feel weepy?	☐	☐	☐	☐
• Smoke?	☐	☐	☐	☐
• Drink alcohol?	☐	☐	☐	☐
• Eat too much?	☐	☐	☐	☐
• Eat when you are not hungry?	☐	☐	☐	☐
• Forget to eat/miss meals?	☐	☐	☐	☐
• Go off your food?	☐	☐	☐	☐
• Feel in a rush?	☐	☐	☐	☐
• Find it difficult to concentrate?	☐	☐	☐	☐
• Not have enough energy to get things done?	☐	☐	☐	☐
• Wake up early?	☐	☐	☐	☐
• Find it difficult to fall asleep?	☐	☐	☐	☐
• Find it difficult to get out of bed in the morning?	☐	☐	☐	☐
• Feel angry?	☐	☐	☐	☐
• Feel you can't cope?	☐	☐	☐	☐
• Find it hard to make decisions?	☐	☐	☐	☐
• Feel sorry for yourself?	☐	☐	☐	☐
• Worry about the future?	☐	☐	☐	☐
• Feel you have lost your sense of humour?	☐	☐	☐	☐
• Take tranquillizers?	☐	☐	☐	☐
• Take non-prescribed drugs?	☐	☐	☐	☐
• Have minor accidents?	☐	☐	☐	☐
• Have emotional outbursts?	☐	☐	☐	☐
• Generally feel upset?	☐	☐	☐	☐

2
Stress and health

Recognizing stress in yourself is only the beginning of coping with it. You may still be hoping that this book's message will be 'it doesn't really matter' or that you can convince yourself 'it's different for me'. For this reason it is useful to consider, albeit briefly, the body's physiological response to stress, and how stress is implicated in certain illnesses.

THE PHYSIOLOGY OF STRESS

The work of Hans Selye, a Canadian endocrinologist, is central to our understanding of the physiology of stress. Selye transformed our approach to stress during the 1930s and 1940s. Much of the work on stress today is based on his ideas and early findings. He proposed a model of stress reaction in the body called the General Adaptation Syndrome (GAS) which has three phases: alarm reaction, resistance and exhaustion.

Alarm reaction

This first reaction is a familiar sensation to everybody, and is best known as the 'fight or flight' response. Put most simply, it means that the body is preparing itself to cope with danger in one of two ways, by fighting or by running away. What causes the problem is that most of the situations we face today which produce this primitive response do not require fighting or running. We are much more likely to have to make a mental response than a bodily one.

The physiological changes required for fighting or running are the same. The hypothalamus in the brain signals to the adrenal glands (over the kidneys), adrenalin is released into the bloodstream, increasing heartbeat, and breathing becomes more shallow. Blood flows from skin and viscera (i.e. the heart, lungs, liver and so on) to muscles and brain taking nourishment, for example, blood sugar, to the parts of the body which will require extra energy for their response to danger. This means the muscles, in particular, which are going to have to either fight or run. As a result of this redistribution we look pale and our hands and feet become cooler. This is why cold hands (in normal temperatures) often indicate anxiety and nervousness. Whilst physiologically the person who turns white is more prepared to fight (the blood having been redistributed to the appropriate muscles), this does not mean that people who are red in the face and blustering will not take a swing at you. They are just not in the best physiological state to do so! Blood pressure is raised and the capillaries of the skin and viscera are narrowed.

These are the sensations that we can feel immediately in our body. It is not, however, all that is going on. Other hormones are also released, notably ACTH (adrenocorticotrophic hormone) which activates the adrenal glands. As a result corticoids are released into the blood stream, carrying messages to other glands and organs.

The spleen, for example, is mobilized to release more red blood cells into the blood stream. These carry oxygen and nourishment and are needed to provide for the extra demands of the body during this alarm stage. The ability of the blood to clot is increased, in preparation for damage resulting from fighting. Vitamins, particularly B and C, and sucrose are released by the liver to be carried to the muscles by the redistributed blood. The stomach releases hydrochloric acid which it only does normally to digest food.

A further response is muscular tension, particularly of the lower back, shoulders and neck and this may result in what is commonly known as a 'tension headache'. Since this tension often remains with us after the other changes due to the alarm reaction have dissipated we come to think of tension as the principle indicator of stress. Noting tension in ourselves or others is a good initial way of measuring or recognizing stress; dealing with tension can be the first step in gaining control.

There is one other hormone released and this is noradrenalin. Whereas adrenalin and cortisone can be seen as the 'anxiety' hormones, noradrenalin brings with it feelings of euphoria and satisfaction—what can be termed 'positive stress'.

The anxiety hormones have been given pre-eminence in most models of stress reaction, including Selye's but some researchers would now see this as an over-emphasis. We know that the continual release of such hormones is bad for us; we are less sure whether 'positive stress' is good for us.

Resistance

In this second stage of stress response the distinctive reactions of the alarm stage fade and disappear, and the body seems to 'return to normal.' At this point we may feel that we have satisfactorily coped with stress. If, however, the stressor persists then the body continues, in fact, to 'fight' it actively and vigorously. Adrenocortical activity is increased and, if the body remains in a state of stress for too long, the resources of the body, such as nutrients and vitamins, will become depleted.

Exhaustion

The body remains in the resistance stage for some time but eventually, if it is still under pressure, new symptoms begin to emerge. These are similar to those shown during the alarm stage. As a result, the body becomes increasingly vulnerable to disease and organic dysfunction of many kinds, and those diseases and conditions we associate with stress begin to show themselves.

If stress is so harmful it seems that we should avoid it. Is this possible? There is no way to avoid it entirely. The alarm stage will be triggered over and over again by a wide range of stimuli, not all of which are negative. Sudden, unexpected excitement or happiness can cause many of the same physiological changes that are also a response to sudden tragedy or disappointment. We might be able to reduce the frequency with which we enter the alarm stage, and its intensity, but we will not be able to eliminate it entirely. Nor should we try to; it is a normal protective mechanism. It is rather that too many of us have a lifestyle which triggers the reaction too often. The resistance stage might also be inevitable to some extent; it is adaptive, the body is programmed to resist disease and stress over periods of time. We should nevertheless try to minimize it because, when stress occurs too often or for too long, the body has no opportunity to recover. After actively fighting stress for some time the body needs to replenish depleted resources, 'to recharge the batteries'. It is when this does not happen that the body enters the last stage, exhaustion, and it is this we are seeking to prevent. What seems to be particularly dangerous is repeated exhaustion. Against this the body stands no chance.

STRESS AND ILLNESS

The World Health Organization takes as a definition for health the presence of physical and emotional well-being in the individual. Stress certainly detracts from the well-being of the individual but does it constitute 'illness'? It is very difficult to link stress clearly as a causal agent in illness but there are a number of areas where it is implicated. In other conditions we know that stress exacerbates the problem, even if, by itself, it does not cause it.

Coronary heart disease is pre-eminent when it comes to considering illness and stress, along with hypertension. Following heart disease the second most common stress-related illnesses are probably those of the alimentary canal, ranging from indigestion to ulcers. Two major problems are peptic ulcers and irritable bowel syndrome. Many people believe that stress is strongly implicated in a number of immunological disorders, and stress may well lower our resistance to infectious diseases of all kinds. It certainly seems to be linked to diabetes mellitus, both in terms of its onset and in the course of the illness. It seems likely that the involvement of stress in diabetes is different for juvenile and maturity onset groups. Other illnesses which may be linked with stress include asthma, some types of cancer, migraine, pre-menstrual tension, rheumatoid arthritis, certain skin disorders and various types of mental and emotional disorders.

The relationship between stress and these illnesses is complex. For example, also implicated in heart disease are diet and lack of exercise as well as too much sudden strenuous exercise, heredity factors, high blood pressure, gross overweight and smoking (which doubles your chances of developing heart disease). There is clearly not space here to enter the debate surrounding each of these conditions.

Checklist 2 looks at the physical signs of stress. The same comments and provisos apply as they did for Checklist 1 (see page 24). Once again, the more 'often' or 'sometimes' categories you have ticked, the more likely you are to be exhibiting signs of stress. Even if you attribute some of your answers to a chronic health problem it may be that this is, itself, a manifestation of stress.

Checklist 2 Physical signs of stress

How often do you experience: Often   Sometimes   Rarely   Never
- Muscle tension?   ☐   ☐   ☐   ☐
- Low back pain?   ☐   ☐   ☐   ☐

	Often	Sometimes	Rarely	Never
● General aches and pains?	☐	☐	☐	☐
● Pains in your shoulders or neck?	☐	☐	☐	☐
● Pains in your chest?	☐	☐	☐	☐
● Stomach/abdominal pain?	☐	☐	☐	☐
● 'Upset stomach', including constipation or diarrhoea?	☐	☐	☐	☐
● Indigestion?	☐	☐	☐	☐
● Muscle spasms or nervous tics?	☐	☐	☐	☐
● Twitching eyelid?	☐	☐	☐	☐
● Fidgeting with your hands, including repetitive movements (e.g. rubbing hands together, fingers picking at one another)?	☐	☐	☐	☐
● General fidgeting (e.g. wriggling, shifting weight from one foot to the other)?	☐	☐	☐	☐
● Shortness of breath, breathlessness?	☐	☐	☐	☐
● Shallow breathing?	☐	☐	☐	☐
● Unexplained rashes or skin irritations?	☐	☐	☐	☐
● Generally itchy skin for no apparent reason?	☐	☐	☐	☐
● Dry mouth in anticipation of events?	☐	☐	☐	☐
● Rapid pulse?	☐	☐	☐	☐
● 'Pounding' or 'racing' of your heart?	☐	☐	☐	☐
● 'Colds', sniffles, runny nose etc?	☐	☐	☐	☐
● Having to keep clearing your throat?	☐	☐	☐	☐
● Headaches?	☐	☐	☐	☐
● Tiredness or lack of energy?	☐	☐	☐	☐
● Loss of interest in sex?	☐	☐	☐	☐
● Dizziness?	☐	☐	☐	☐

	Often	Sometimes	Rarely	Never
● Nausea?	☐	☐	☐	☐
● Sweaty palms?	☐	☐	☐	☐
● Sweating when you are not physically active?	☐	☐	☐	☐
● 'Butterflies' in your stomach?	☐	☐	☐	☐

II
What causes stress?

3
Stress and lifestyle

In describing stress in their life, many people see it as an excess of demands over resources, and when they look to see where these demands come from, concentrate on pressures from outside. Stress is something which is 'done to us'. This is only part of the story. Pressures, or stressors, also come from within, from our beliefs, attitudes and expectations about the world and ourselves, from our habits and behaviour, and from our personality. Even the stressors from 'out there' fall into different groups: physical, environmental stressors, such as noise and pollution; cultural expectations; and more personal social expectations from family and friends, boss and colleagues.

Some people have more stressors in their natural environment than others. It might be especially important for such people not to add to this load. Because of personality or other factors some will be more at risk than others, either all the time or at particular points in their lives. These people may also need to be especially careful not to overload themselves. We will consider a range of 'at risk' variables.

PERSONALITY TYPE

Type A personalities (see pages 45-57) and those who are particularly prone to worry and anxiety may be at more risk than others from stress and stress-related illnesses. This will be considered in the next chapter.

LIFE EVENTS

The work of two Americans, Holmes and Rahe, has indicated the importance of 'life events' to our health. They are, for the most part, 'normal' events which occur to most of us over a lifetime, and which change our lives or lifestyle in some way. The emphasis here is on change—the events themselves can be positive or negative. Lists of life events include both exits and entrances to the family: for example, death, divorce, or children leaving home would be considered exits while marriage and birth are entrances to the family. Other events would include changing your job in some way, either through moving, promotion, redundancy or retirement, moving house, new friends, taking a holiday and so on. This analysis makes no attempt to find out how you as an individual rate these events, or whether you see them as positive or negative.

Research suggests that experiencing an excessive number of life events in a particular period of time will lead to increased ill health. The length of time such events take to have a physical impact seems to vary with particular illnesses. The variety of illnesses linked with life events is wide, ranging from breast cancer to depression, but the mechanism by which this volume of change affects the body has not yet been explained.

These changes cannot be avoided for the most part and, because many are positive, they should not be. We can neither stop people dying nor would we want to stop people marrying and having children. What is important, however, is to try to minimize the number of life events that occur in a short time. This may not always be easy. If, for example, you are getting married and this involves leaving home, moving away from the area where you have always lived, away from family, friends and job, and settling in another part of the country in a new job, your life is clearly undergoing a major upheaval. No matter how much you want all of this it takes time to adjust to the changes. It might be helpful to avoid other, unnecessary changes and to look after your general health as much as possible.

If you can, it is generally wise to avoid unnecessary additional changes when you have had a major life event. For example, changing your job when you divorce or are widowed can add dramatically to the amount of stress experienced and to your difficulty in coping with the situation.

DAILY EVENTS

For most of us life events are fairly rare, though major, occurrences in our lives. Most of us do not get married more than once or twice, have more than two or three children, or change jobs or houses frequently and, although there may be a tendency for these events to cluster, they are events most of us take in our stride.

For many people, it is the small daily events which cause the most stress. We can all think of a seemingly trivial happening which turned out to be the last straw. An American psychologist, Lazarus, and his colleagues have carried out research in this area, devising a scale to measure what they call 'daily hassles and uplifts'. Many events appear both as possible 'hassles' and 'uplifts'. This is because most events are neutral; how we rate them depends on our attitude, what else is going on, what we want to do and so forth. So not only does the impact of an event vary between people, it can vary within the individual over time. The wet weather that prevents your longed-for picnic may also be a blessing if it means you do not have to mow the lawn.

BELIEFS AND ATTITUDES

We keep coming back to the idea that it is our attitude to an event which matters more than the event itself. In part III, when we consider ways of coping with stress, we will constantly be challenging your assumptions and considering how you can adjust them. Our thinking is as much governed by habit as by behaviour and changing our thinking habits is as difficult as altering our behaviour. It can be done, however, with enough motivation and practice.

There is one particular school of psychotherapy, founded by Albert Ellis, called rational-emotive therapy, whose aim is to change the way you think about yourself and the world. A major contention is that we live by assumptions or beliefs which are irrational, which affect our opinions and expectations of ourselves, others and the world in general. Ellis cites a number of basic, and common, irrational beliefs that most of us have. They can be summarized in three basic groups. The first focuses on ourselves, and runs along the lines of, 'I must be right, outstanding, pleasing, accepted and loved—and if I'm not, then its awful, unbearable and I'm no good or worthless for failing'. The second group looks at our assumptions about other people, and suggests we believe that, 'Other people must do things my way and give me what I want—and if they do not then it's awful and unbearable and they are no good or worthless for not pleasing me'. The last group centres on our view of what life should be like and encompasses the belief that, 'Life must be easy, painless, guaranteed and give me all (if not more than) I want—and if it does not then it's awful and unbearable and life is no good for depressing me'.

Many of our beliefs need to be examined in detail and taken further than usual before we begin to see how irrational they really are. Most of us would accept that a common belief or desire is to be liked by others. On the surface this is acceptable, but when it turns into 'I must be liked (or loved, or approved of) by everybody I meet', we can see how it is becoming irrational. We need to ask ourselves, is this possible? Is it desirable? What are the consequences of this belief?

We are all familiar with the idea, attributed to both Phineas Barnum and Abraham Lincoln, that 'You can fool all the people most of the time, and some of the people all of the time, but you cannot fool all the people all the time.' The same is true of being liked. Some people will like us some of the time and some will never like us. There is nothing we can do to ensure that everyone likes us all the time.

When we think about it we can see that the belief is nonsensical, irrational. No matter what you do, think or say, *someone* will dislike it. Take this irrational belief further. Suppose you have one hundred people who do like and approve of you, can you bask in this warm feeling? No, because you are worried about the one hundred and first person who might not like you. This belief condemns you to never being able to enjoy the positive feelings of those who do like you fully, because you are too busy worrying about those who do not. Furthermore, do you really want to be liked, approved of, by everybody? What about the people *you* do not like or approve of?

Coupled with this belief system is the notion that if your expectations are not fulfilled then it's awful, unbearable, the end of the world. Whilst it might be sad or unpleasant if someone does not like you (and you like them), it is hardly likely to be the end of everything. We have yet to find out what that is. As far as individuals go, death is the literal end of this world. Is not being liked by someone really going to bring us to 'the end'?

We will return again and again to the concept of irrational beliefs and how they colour our thinking, emotions and behaviour. Learning to challenge our own belief system is not easy but when we experience a negative emotion, be it stress, anxiety, depression, or whatever, we should always ask ourselves the following questions:

- What am I saying to myself at the moment?
- What belief is this based on?
- What assumptions am I making?
- Are these assumptions reasonable, rational?
- What are the real consequences of believing this?
- What will *really* happen if I do not get what I want or my belief is not fulfilled?

You do not *have* to change your belief system, your irrational ideas. The choice is yours. All I am suggesting to you is that certain assumptions, beliefs or expectations bring with them certain specifiable negative consequences. If you are prepared to accept the anxiety, uncertainty and worry about yourself which goes with wanting to be liked by everyone then you can continue to want this. Where the real problem lies is wanting this (because, as you say, 'everyone does' or 'it's only natural') but *not* wanting the negative feelings that come with it. You cannot have it both ways.

It is only 'natural' that most of us consider what we believe or assume to be firstly, believed by most other people and secondly, right! This means we may be very resistant to changing our beliefs. To assist this process it is often useful to question where a belief or attitude comes from. Why do we believe some of the irrational things we do? In many cases what gave rise to the belief in the first place may not matter—it may be enough to realize that we hold it, and that it is unreasonable. But we may use its origins as a reason to hang on to it. If, for example, we say 'it is only natural' or 'it is only normal' to want to be liked by everyone, then we may be less happy about changing this belief. After all, who wants to be unnatural or abnormal?

We assume this belief arises spontaneously in all our minds, but its seeds lie in our culture and are reinforced by the way we are treated as children, our parents' beliefs, our friends' beliefs, the sort of books we read, and so on.

The origins of other beliefs can be seen more immediately. We push ourselves hard at work because our boss expects it. Our concept of what it means to be a good wife or husband is in part based on our spouse's expectations. In such cases it will be necessary to take the source of the assumption into account—but that still does not make the belief right; and are you sure—*really* sure—that you know what the other person believes?

There is not space here to question the origins of beliefs but overcoming irrational beliefs and expectations is central to managing stress well.

SOCIAL SUPPORT

A listening ear when we need to pour out our troubles is essential to everyone. If it comes attached to someone we care about and who cares about us, so much the better. And if it brings with it a sympathetic manner, support, comfort, a helping hand, praise, sensible advice or whatever is needed, then you are very lucky and have a major asset in managing stress.

Most people will look to their partners for support but where there is no partner, other family and friends can be just as supportive, sometimes even more so. Talking over a specific problem with someone in the same situation may be more useful, in terms of real understanding, insight and helpful suggestions, than a caring, well-meaning spouse or friend who does not fully realize your anxieties. To have this generalized support in the background is invaluable, nevertheless.

Our mobile society forces many people to move away from family, friends and traditional sources of support. This sort of support can be created—everyone should have some support system, whether it be a partner or a group of friends. To derive most benefit from a support system, however, it must be mutual—you have to give as well as take.

MEANING IN LIFE

Finding meaning in life is a task which is never fully completed, and to expect it to be so only adds to your pressures. But to have some idea of what is important to you, what your values are, and what life is about in the long run is necessary for all of us. Whether this is couched in terms of philosophy, religion or morals, it gives a framework for existence which gives life meaning, makes sense of daily activities and can help put stresses into perspective. No one can manufacture a belief in something merely as a way of alleviating stress but belief in nothing means you are faced with the question 'What is the point?' This is likely to exacerbate any stresses or other negative feelings you are already experiencing. You may not have an answer but to be searching for one is the next best thing.

ENVIRONMENTAL STRESSORS

There is one group of factors which causes us stress and which has little or nothing to do with our attitude. These are physical or environmental stressors, and include such factors as noise, pollution, light, overcrowding and the like. These are things which we know cause bodily changes, which for the most part we can quantify; whether we are aware of them or not, whether we see them as negative or positive, makes no difference to the physical impact they have. Of course, we might add to our subjective feelings of stress, and ultimately worsen our bodily condition, by what we think about the events.

For example, there is no question that noise reduces performance (through clouding judgement, decreasing efficiency, reducing precision and making us irritable and bad-tempered) and can cause permanent hearing loss. This has nothing to do with where the noise comes from, or whether we choose it or not. The sound of a pneumatic drill hammering away is psychologically unpleasant and physically painful for most people. Compare this to the painful level of noise at a rock concert or disco, which most young people would approve of—'It's *supposed* to sound like that,' 'You can feel the music.' Whether it's supposed to sound like that or not, the level of noise is still causing physical stress, in the form of hearing damage.

In a work situation we may have little control over some of these factors, and factory and other industrial laws may not be sufficient to ensure as stress-free a physical working environment as many of us would like. There are some things, however, that you might be able to deal with as an individual or as part of a group within an office. Other issues will need organizational input and change. Specific areas will be dealt with in chapter 5.

STRESS AS NECESSARY MOTIVATION

As was shown in chapter 2, some stress or arousal is necessary to get us to do anything. A certain amount provides an incentive to do things—indeed, to do anything—and more induces us to perform better. All this is true up to a certain point, the point when arousal, in a sense, becomes stress.

In our jobs a number of incentives influence us, including the need to earn money and the need to find some satisfaction in our work. These basic needs are quickly sub-divided and then become forgotten in a welter of smaller, sometimes conflicting, desires. We want to earn not just enough money to live comfortably, but more, to provide for luxuries (which quickly become necessities). We want not just our own approval for a job well done, but that of our bosses, colleagues and compatriots in the wider industry. We become increasingly ambitious, demanding more of ourselves, and are not always sure when we have reached our goals. Children at school receive coloured stars for work well done. In our jobs many of us are chasing gold stars which never come; we have forgotten that the system has stopped awarding them.

I am not for a moment suggesting that all ambition is a bad thing but, like everything else, it should be pursued in a healthy, rational and enjoyable way—not in an unhealthy, irrational fashion which will only help you towards your first early heart attack.

Why some people seem to feel the need to push themselves to the limit and beyond has a number of explanations, but some relate to our belief in the motivational nature of stress. 'I work better under pressure' is usually a mistaken belief. If you can only put your mind to doing something when the deadline looms then you should be questioning your whole method of working and your attitude to that piece of work. Maybe you need the pressure of a deadline because you are using it like a stick—you do not really want to do the work at all. If you have always assumed the deadline was a carrot, this is an important reversal in thinking.

Taking the belief in 'pressure' further, some people, indeed some occupations, seem to prize stress. It becomes synonymous with their profession or industry. Stress is no longer just pressure but has metamorphosed into stimulus and thence to challenge, excitement, adventure and even glamour.

Stress as glamour

Individuals and industries may consider stress as something glamorous but the thinking behind it is still dangerous, as is the behaviour espoused: overwork to the point of inefficiency or incompetence, haste to the point of lethargy, working long hours to the point of exhaustion, hype to the point of disbelief, all accompanied by too much alcohol, smoking and poor dietary habits. Individuals in any organization may embrace this type of lifestyle in the belief that being constantly on the move, never having time, having too much to do makes them look more important. It might make them appear so to those misguided by the same belief; to others they simply appear inefficient, incompetent or downright foolish.

It is essentially an old-fashioned belief system that allows you to think that having an ulcer or a heart attack is a demonstration of your commitment to your career and of your significance. Apart from the damage it does you personally, it harms your company too. You have time off work, your firm has to pay you for being unproductive and someone else has to be paid to do your work. Even if you are not ill enough to take time off, you will not be working efficiently. More and more people are coming round to the belief that it is possible to accomplish a great deal, to be ambitious, to achieve their goals, and to do so healthily and to enjoy it. The nature of some occupations may inevitably involve working long hours or deadlines. Journalists clearly have a paper to get out on time. Junior doctors work ludicrously long hours. Executives have to take crucial and often difficult decisions. These are intrinsic to the job and are challenges to be met sensibly. Adding drink or drugs, for example, aggravates the problem, rather than solving it. Fighting against the tide of common assumptions about how, for example, a journalist should behave is not always easy. It is not helped by the image professionals choose to project in the media. It is one thing for a drama series on television to portray the stresses of life in particular occupations, quite another when this is assumed to be a prerequisite. An apparently serious article on advertising in a women's magazine laid down the 'key requirements' for working in this field (*Working Woman*, March 1986). It might be reasonable to include a 'taste for long hours' but to suggest that 'last, but not least, a high alcohol threshold' seems nothing short of irresponsible.

MEN, WOMEN AND STRESS

Who are more stressed, men or women? For the individual it does not really matter; what matters is *your* level of stress and *your* ability to cope. It will be of importance, however, if much of your stress stems from being a member of a social group which is under pressure because of the expectations put on it by society in general. It is like asking who is more stressed: the middle-class person struggling to find the money to send the children to a private school, or the low-paid worker struggling to keep the family warm and fed? The latter's needs may be more fundamental and can thus be seen as more important, but it does not help the former with his or her dilemma.

Part of the difficulty arises from what we mean by stress, how we measure it and what we see as 'allowable'. People do not stop thinking they have financial problems because others think they have a good income. And it should be remembered that most women, like men, work from economic necessity and not for 'pin-money'.

As far as measuring stress in men and women is concerned, both sides believe that the situation is better for the opposite sex, but clearly both groups do experience stress. Many causes are held in common; a number are peculiar to each sex. How stress is expressed differs between the sexes and is conditioned by society. Women are more likely to turn to tranquillizers, men to alcohol. Women are more likely to have mental and emotional problems, men physical ones. This is still true despite some evidence to suggest the patterns are changing slowly. For example, alcohol problems are on the increase among women, as are cardio-vascular problems. It is not really possible to measure which sex is more stressed, except on a very subjective level.

Having said that, it is important to realize that some groups are more at risk than others. We have already covered some danger areas in this chapter, but it must also be recognized that working mothers and single parents (the majority of whom are women) are likely to fall into a high-risk group. They have demands made on them from two separate sources, and this has to be acknowledged. There are practical problems which society and employers can help with—for example, more and better day-care facilities for children, more flexible hours, job-sharing, easier return to work after child-rearing and so forth. Other difficulties, such as general attitudes to workers and expectations of what being a 'good mother' means, may require rethinking by the collective mind but more immediately they require dealing with by the individual concerned.

4
Stress and personality

Whenever one talks of the 'stress-prone individual' or the 'stress-personality' one is almost certainly referring to what is called the 'Type A personality'. Researchers divide people into Type A or Type B and then demonstrate that various illnesses, notably heart attacks, are more prevalent amongst Type A people than Type B. This is worrying if you are Type A, particularly if you are happy to be that way or believe you *need* to be like that to be successful at your job.

Quickly reading down a list of aspects of Type A behaviour can give a stereotyped picture of a Type A person which is unattractive, so we tend to believe we are not like that, that these characteristics do not apply to us. We may believe that we are Type A but we will be the one to survive and reach the top, or that that is the way we are and have to be, and there is nothing we can do about it. Is that all the research comes down to—either you are Type A and stress-prone, or not?

The time has come to examine Type A behaviour more closely.

ARE YOU TYPE A?

Before reading further, answer the questions in Checklist 3 (overleaf) as honestly as possible. The questions describe different aspects of behaviour. Rate how each applies to you using the rating scale 0-6, where 6 is 'could not describe me better', 0 is 'complete opposite to me', and 3 is neutral.

Checklist 3 Type A behaviour

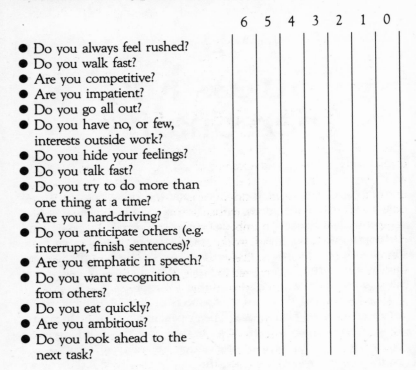

6 5 4 3 2 1 0

- Do you always feel rushed?
- Do you walk fast?
- Are you competitive?
- Are you impatient?
- Do you go all out?
- Do you have no, or few, interests outside work?
- Do you hide your feelings?
- Do you talk fast?
- Do you try to do more than one thing at a time?
- Are you hard-driving?
- Do you anticipate others (e.g. interrupt, finish sentences)?
- Are you emphatic in speech?
- Do you want recognition from others?
- Do you eat quickly?
- Are you ambitious?
- Do you look ahead to the next task?

Your total will be in the range from 0 to 96. The higher the score you have, the more typical of Type A you are; the lower your score, the more typical of Type B. Many people will be neither dramatically one nor the other but will fall towards the middle, with one type predominating. Rather than look at absolute scores, see your score as falling in a particular group (see Fig 2). Around the 48 mark you are neither one type nor the other. As you move along the scale you become

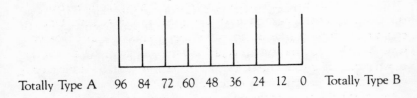

Totally Type A   96 84 72 60 48 36 24 12 0   Totally Type B

Fig 2

more typical of Type A or Type B. Thus at 60 you are pushing your way towards being Type A, whereas at 72 you are definitely in the Type A camp.

This is not always an easy questionnaire to answer, particularly in the middle ranges, and it is easy to convince ourselves we are less like Type A than we really are. Before we consider how we manage this, let us look further at the description of Type A behaviour.

TYPE A BEHAVIOUR

The term Type A comes to us from the work of the American cardiologists Friedman and Roseman who were prominent in the 1950s and who still work in this field. The typical picture of a Type A is one of a person who is hard-driving and demanding, both of self and others. He or she is ambitious, particularly in the material sense, highly competitive, works at a number of different tasks at the same time and constantly looks ahead, works under pressure of time and always seems rushed. He/she is likely to be aggressive, critical, hostile, undemonstrative, less interested in family than work, and more likely to blame others or external circumstances when things go wrong or goals are frustrated.

This is not the most attractive character sketch we could make yet there can be positive aspects to Type A. Such people often have a high degree of mental and/or physical alertness and can accomplish a great deal, carrying others along with their enthusiasm and drive.

Many young executives striving to reach the top of their career ladder believe they must behave like this if they are to accomplish anything and get ahead. Many accounts of the Type A person lead us to see him (usually described as him, which is in itself misleading) as the 'executive type', out to reach the top. This makes it easy to assume we are not Type A if we do not fit into the corporate executive mould and are not striving for material success, but it is possible to behave in a Type A way in other settings.

It is a mistake to believe that it is only the hard-driving, strongly competitive, rushed, aggressive person who gets things done. Type Bs can often achieve just as much—only they go about it in a different way. Whether you measure success by what you have, what you do or what you are is your choice. But whatever you want, there are more, as well as less, healthy ways of achieving it.

By considering some of the major characteristics of Type A behaviour we can examine where they come from, the guises in which they appear and whether they are really necessary.

Being under pressure of time

Being under time pressure means that you usually feel rushed or hurried and never have enough time for the things you must do, let alone the things you want to do. It leads to feeling irritated and impatient, especially with other people or things around you. You end up trying to hurry others in their behaviour—which can range from interrupting a person and finishing his sentence for him to sitting on someone's tail in the motorway fast lane, flashing your lights.

In trying to do more and more in less and less time you end up doing two things at once—dictating or shaving while driving, reading and watching the television, talking on the telephone and punching figures into a computer, reading and eating, talking business and playing golf. The list is endless. At times we all think of one thing whilst doing another, but for the Type A person it is a way of life.

An alternative or adjunct to doing more than one thing at a time is to set unrealistic deadlines. It goes with the 'I want it yesterday' approach, the belief that you can work a bit faster, a bit longer. It is the 'God took six days to create the world—I'll do it in five-and-a-half' mentality.

Packing more events or tasks into less time inevitably means making fewer allowances for the unforeseen. Whether this is falling ill, a mechanical breakdown in vital equipment or an act of God, you have no leeway in your schedule. It also means not allowing for occurrences which you can and should foresee. *Traffic travels slower in the rush hour.* This is a fact of life instantly apparent to all commuters on day one but, nevertheless, many people retire never really having believed it. They act as though becoming angry, frustrated, irritable or hostile will suddenly open up new roads so traffic can flow more freely.

The major hurdle to overcome is the belief that time pressure is a positive thing. It often does spur you on to do more—but in the short term only. Some things require your whole attention and to give them less results in errors or miscalculations. These have to be rectified, taking up more time.

Habitually working long hours may mean we are tired and sluggish, and cannot concentrate. Again, we make mistakes or the task takes longer than it would, or could, if we were fresh. We become irritable with others and vent our bad temper on them. As a result they are less inclined to be helpful or to put themselves out for us and we may find ourselves waiting for information to reach us, work to be completed, or reports to be typed.

In the long run, being constantly rushed and pushed to get work done ceases to be a challenge or an incentive and becomes a relentless grind. At this point we are inefficient, possibly even incompetent, and any extra buzz we may have felt from pushing ourselves has long gone. Type A behaviour has ceased to be productive.

Time pressure can also show itself in general irritation and impatience with things, with others and with yourself. Waiting for anything is intolerable and you can even be irritable with yourself when you have to do repetitive tasks, or tasks you consider boring or unnecessary which stop you doing what you really want to do. With some people this can go as far as resenting any time not spent on work or on achieving their main objective—including time spent socializing or even time spent asleep. Things are postponed as you find it difficult to 'make time' for everyday chores and necessities—be it finding time for lunch or having your hair cut.

By planning time better, learning what it is realistic to expect and what is best left to the Almighty it is possible to achieve as much with less wasted effort and energy and, furthermore, to feel fit and happy at the end of it. The specific skills required for dealing with time pressure are laid out in chapter 9.

Egoism

Type As are typically egocentric, focused inward on their own wants, needs and wishes. They have little time for other people, particularly their problems and difficulties, and have no patience if things do not go as they want. They may express superficial concern but do not alter their behaviour. They simply do not want to be inconvenienced. If a colleague or subordinate complains about their work load—too much, badly prepared, impossible deadlines, or whatever—the Type A person will show surprise, possibly concern, may trot out a few well-worn clichés about the complainant's value, profer a bunch of flowers or an after-work drink, but take no notice.

Type As generally only offer praise or notice others when backed into a corner. On a daily basis it simply does not occur to them to do so. They are, however, much more open-handed with their criticism and blame. Unaware of not caring that their work habits affect others, they continue to work in ways which have negative consequences for others. That these back-up staff may be lower-paid subordinates, who are not in a position to achieve the same job satisfaction as themselves, is ignored. They are essentially taking advantage, either ruthlessly or through unthinking blindness, of high levels of unemployment and lack of opportunity to change jobs to treat staff poorly.

If they are told this they will usually exhibit surprise and disbelief. Convinced of their own rightness in all things they simply cannot conceive of anyone objecting to the way they work. High turnover of staff may be due to the job itself—it is either too pressured, too boring or too plain nasty—but most frequently it is due to poor management and an impossible boss.

The inability of Type As to see their own shortcomings or to accept that they might be wrong leads them to look outside themselves for someone or something to blame when things go wrong. They can be extremely inventive in this search. If necessary, but usually as a last resort, they will blame their competitors, or the trade unions. Failing these they will blame fate or a malevolent deity—anything rather than admit they have made a less than optimal decision.

The self-preoccupation of Type A individuals leads them to ignore their environment as well as other people. They notice little of what goes on around them unless it is immediately revelant, and show little— if any—interest in the aesthetics of their surroundings.

Competitiveness

Many Type As do not feel alive, let alone happy, unless they are locked into competition with someone or something. It is as though they feel compelled to challenge one another, almost regardless of the circumstances. To win is one of the hallmarks of success, and is frequently a motivator more powerful than anything else.

These are the people who obsessively check out how others are doing, measuring themselves on the yardstick of others' performances. This can be linked with highly egocentric behaviour and their outlook can become highly biased towards the individual, losing sight entirely of the larger goals of the group. At the extreme, such people find it hard to act as a member of a team, whether it is in the office or the sports field. They alone must shine—and this gets in the way of being co-operative where it is appropriate.

Being highly competitive usually ends up bringing out the worst in people rather than the best. Such people fall into the egocentric trap of not liking to see others do well. The real objectives may be lost from sight as the subsidiary goal of simply 'beating the other person' takes over. Trivial factors and events will assume a significance which in the overall pattern they do not deserve. Seeking to make the other person look 'bad' or incompetent ends up exercising your imagination more than finding ways to achieve your objectives. This can lead to destructive acts ranging from failing to pass on messages and getting the time of the meeting or a phone number just slightly wrong, to acts of outright sabotage. Such behaviour tends ultimately to be self-defeating. It is not only your 'rival' but the company who has lost an opportunity, contract, account, or whatever. If you persist in such behaviour you eventually become known as untrustworthy—either inadvertently or maliciously so, depending on the generosity or competitiveness of the person doing the labelling.

Being competitive can lead you into becoming increasingly aggressive and hostile in your interaction with others. Your conversational tone becomes one that is generally challenging and few people will choose to have anything to do with you. Fine, you may say, work is about work and getting things done, not about socializing but look at it from other people's point of view. If you are unrewarding to deal with, known to guard your information jealously and not pass it on or share ideas, why should they do anything to help you? They might not start out being as competitive as you but you can back people into a corner where they will be deliberately unhelpful, even if, on occasions, it damages them. Or they will form cliques, seeking to exclude someone who will never share or co-operate. Alexis Carrington Colby and J.R. Ewing might be powerful figures in a fantasy world, but glamorizing ruthless competition to the point of out-and-out revenge, unethical behaviour, or borderline criminality will not work in the real work place.

Some companies seem to go out of their way to encourage competition. Sales departments in particular compare accounts between individuals and may even go so far as to have charts displaying sales figures and prizes offered at regular intervals. 'Employee of the month' schemes also offer prizes, but usually do not spell out the criteria by which people are judged. It is a case of doing your job 'better' or 'superbly well', for which you are rewarded. The latter is thus harder to judge how well you are doing, but also easier to ignore.

Some people respond well, at least superficially, to this type of imposed competition; others find it stressful and inhibiting. Such people do not need imposed 'motivation' to do a good job. Indeed, they are more likely to work better in co-operation or for the satisfaction of making the sale. And so on. They may see each sale as a competition between themselves and the buyer but not want actively to compete with colleagues—after all, everyone wants what is best for the firm, maximum sales.

There are occasions when an element of competition is inevitable. Applying for a job or for promotion may lead to being 'in competition' with other people for the post. In such situations it is easy to confuse competition with self-promotion. The two may be connected in some instances but they are not the same.

How can we tell when competition has ceased to serve a useful motivating function and has become excessive? Straightforward guidelines include checking whether you spend more time acting negatively—i.e. damaging others, than you do positively—i.e. seeking solutions to the real problems, achieving the stated goals, and positively promoting yourself. Also, examine whether competition is taking over your life—do you *have* to be the first away at the traffic lights? Do you always *have* to win—even if you are playing snakes and ladders with your children? If you are competing, even when you are supposedly relaxing, you have problems. We have all heard of the person who drops dead whilst jogging, playing squash, or taking some other form of exercise—exercise, furthermore, which is usually undertaken to improve cardiovascular functioning and resilience. Such people usually set themselves unrealistic targets, to be achieved in too short a time, or compete against people younger than themselves. A fit 50-year-old may run faster than an unfit 30-year-old but will not beat a fit 30. Schoolboys can beat women's athletic records. Choosing sensible standards is important.

This takes us back to the importance of irrational ideas and unrealistic expectations. If you are 30, no matter how good your tennis, you are not suddenly going to win Wimbledon. Most of us can accept this. Applying the same *realistic* criteria to work ambitions need not stifle them but can be used positively to achieve what is possible, rather than frustratedly chasing the impossible.

Why do you need to compete, to win? Are your concepts of self-worth based on the irrational notion that if you are not first nothing counts? If competing and winning are ends in themselves then you probably need to review your ideas about yourself and your life as outlined in chapter 3. If, however, competition is only the means to a greater end—namely, success of some kind, be it more money, promotion, fame—then you need to consider whether other strategies might not bring you closer to your goal with less stress to yourself and others.

Finally, there is the group of people who dismiss any tendency towards seeing themselves as Type A saying 'But I am not competitive.' They will say that they have no need to measure themselves against others to see how well they are doing. They know they are doing well or even very well, and monitor present performance against their own past performance. This can certainly get you away from the notion of competing against others and needing to sabotage them, but can still set up intolerable competitive pressures, be it running that bit faster or further than last time or selling that bit more. You cannot always beat yourself. It may be important to review your answer to the question about being competitive, and consider how much you hold your own past record to be 'the competition'.

Ambition

Just as we need to reassess what is meant by being competitive so should we examine what we mean by being ambitious. 'I'm not ambitious,' you may say confidently, meaning that you do not want to climb a corporate—or any sort of—ladder. 'I'm not seeking material success.' The ambition of the Type A person has been traditionally defined in these ways with other types of aspiration either ignored or implicitly approved. Maybe there is something in this; some ambitions may seem more worthwhile than others, have more social impact, are in some way better. Nevertheless, it seems possible that the most altruistic ambitions can be pursued in a way which is clearly stress-prone.

It is easy to assume that because you have opted out of a rat-race job your ambitions are therefore acceptable and will not cause you problems. This may be so but not necessarily. Whether your ambitions centre on money and material success, on acquiring more knowledge, or on righting social injustices are philosophical and ethical choices for you to make. It is how you achieve these ambitions as much as what they are that will be reflected in your health. Academics are unlikely to be seeking success in financial and material terms (or if they are, they have already added to their problems by choosing a comparatively low-paid profession) but may be ambitious in terms of the number of papers and books they publish, the amount of research grants they obtain and thus the number of research assistants they have.

Ambition is not a bad thing in itself and clearly we would never progress if we did not set out to achieve things, but if ambition is pursued to the exclusion of all else, then it is likely to be harmful to the individual. Even people working for the most altruistic ends must occasionally ask whether sacrificing themselves is worth it. If the answer to that is yes, he may still be sacrificing himself to his work in an inefficient way which leaves him burnt out and washed up (to mix images and metaphors) long before necessary.

Typically the over-ambitious person is hard-driving to the point where relaxing is considered unproductive and doing 'nothing' involves guilt feelings. This is linked to feelings of being under pressure of time. Sleeping becomes something that can be cut down because it achieves nothing. Meals are either skipped or eaten on the move, if they are not large, unhealthy business lunches. People who behave like this generally would not dream of treating their car in the same way. Staying physically fit means being more productive, not less. And staying healthy (see chapter 7) includes being able to relax and to take some time out from work.

Going away for the weekend is *not* a relaxing experience if you dictate in the car as you drive there and back, spend most of the day catching up on reading reports or technical journals and spend the evening with a colleague or client who 'just happens to live out this way'. Reading a novel instead of a report may not suit everyone but don't forget there is an incredible world of subjects other than your own to read about, or music to listen to, or art to involve yourself in, or games to play. Even, dare I say it, family to be with.

Self-worth

Much of the behaviour of the Type A person brings us back to asking how we assess ourselves. As we saw in chapter 3, the criteria by which we measure our self-worth may not always be the most rational.

The Type A person seems to be saying 'I am only worth what I achieve', or 'I am only worth what I own', or 'I am only worth while when I win.' Winning is often equated with being in control and the Type A individual wants to be in control. Always and against all odds.

Such beliefs and behaviour can lead to self-doubt and increased pressure. It can also lead to seeking to place the blame for things that go wrong outside yourself. Is it logical to believe that when things go right it is always due to you, but when they go wrong, never? Some Type As seem to believe this implicitly. Apart from being somewhat illogical, always blaming others can lead to a breakdown in co-operative working relationships as people leave you to manage on your own. If what they contribute is not evaluated realistically (i.e. you take all the credit and off-load all the blame, regardless of where ideas come from) why should they go out of their way to be helpful?

The people who go on being helpful in such circumstances are usually in subordinate servile roles and will often define 'taking the blame' as one of the duties of their job. If they can distance themselves from this role, and not take it personally, they will survive it. If not, it will lead to frustration, indignation, resentfulness and depression. Their sense of self-worth will have been constantly undermined by the negative process of being used as a scapegoat, being blamed.

Assessing self-worth goes beyond surface questioning to challenge fundamental beliefs, not only about yourself but about the way you view the world, the nature of man and what you think about religious and philosophical truths. Explaining these is outside the scope of this book, but investigate them—even if only superficially—and look at the logical outcome of your beliefs. Are you setting up a 'no-win' scenario? Do you honestly want to believe in a no-win world?

THE ANXIOUS PERSON

Earlier we noted that anxiety had many characteristics in common with an acute stress state. Just as we cannot escape all stress, we cannot escape all anxiety. The key question is, is your anxiety appropriate? By this I mean are you anxious about the right things, in the right proportions, at the right time? Being phobic would be an example of disproportionate anxiety caused by an object which would not normally provoke such a reaction.

Some people seem to exhibit anxiety as a personality trait. This means they experience anxiety or worry for much of the time. Every change in their life brings anxiety, rather than feelings of challenge or excitement. Such people are usually well known as 'worriers' and they are often highly talented and creative in finding things to worry about. Coupled with this is usually a general sense of pessimism—after all, it is hard to be optimistic when everything that happens is worthy of worry.

We all know people like this. They are the ones who worry when things are going badly (they might get worse) and who worry when things are going well (what is around the corner). If things are going really well they worry that it is all going *too* well and if there is nothing to worry about, they worry about that.

Trying to talk such people out of their worry is usually a non-starter. Their whole way of life is geared to viewing the world in this particular way. Encouraging them to reassess their beliefs, as described in chapter 3, may help.

Sometimes anxiety which is persistent and not related to any particular object or experience is termed 'free-floating anxiety'. In a mild form it may be connected with habitual ways of thinking and behaving. It might be hard but such people have to learn to see the jug as half-full rather than half-empty. Some people see 'feeling happy' as a state which is attached to certain events or conditions, rather than an optimistic way of approaching life. 'Free-floating joy' is an important concept in an individual's ability to resist stress.

NON-ASSERTIVE BEHAVIOUR

People who are non-assertive, whether generally or in particular circumstances (for example, at work), may experience increased stress through feelings of resentment, frustration, being put-upon and a sense of inadequacy and inability to do what they want. It is discussed further in chapter 10.

STRESS-PRONE CHARACTERISTICS

From the foregoing sections we can see that there is another type of person, as well as the hard-driving Type A, who might be seen as stress-prone. This person is likely to be negative in his outlook, anxious and/or generally tense, and possibly non-assertive, feeling that his life and environment are out of control.

Checklist 4 looks at these characteristics. As in the earlier questionnaires there are no absolute scores, but the more frequently you answer 'often', the more stress-prone you are. The questions describe aspects of thinking. Rate how each applies to you. The purpose of the questionnaire is to help give you an insight into where your problems lie and some of the sources of your faulty thinking, rather than to give a definite probability as to the likelihood of your becoming severely stressed.

Checklist 4 Stress-prone characteristics

	Often	Sometimes	Rarely	Never
● Do you think of yourself as less worthwhile than others?	☐	☐	☐	☐
● Do you find yourself thinking pessimistically about yourself?	☐	☐	☐	☐
● Do you find yourself thinking pessimistically about life in general, the world?	☐	☐	☐	☐
● Do you feel as though you have little control over your life?	☐	☐	☐	☐
● When a number of things go wrong at one time do you feel overwhelmed?	☐	☐	☐	☐
● Do you feel trapped or anxious when unforeseen incidents intrude on your day?	☐	☐	☐	☐

	Often	Sometimes	Rarely	Never
• Do you see change as a burden or an obstacle to be overcome?	☐	☐	☐	☐
• Do you feel tense or anxious for no good reason?	☐	☐	☐	☐
• Do you tend to be over-serious or gloomy?	☐	☐	☐	☐
• Do you find yourself doing things you do not want to do?	☐	☐	☐	☐
• Do you find yourself missing out on things you want to do?	☐	☐	☐	☐
• Do you blame other people, circumstances or 'fate' when things go wrong?	☐	☐	☐	☐
• Do you credit other people, circumstances or 'fate' when things go well?	☐	☐	☐	☐
• Do you feel 'put-upon'?	☐	☐	☐	☐
• Are your goals for work vague?	☐	☐	☐	☐
• Do you feel you know what you want out of life?				

5
Stress at work

Stress is often defined as an excess of demands over the individual's ability to meet them. We have all experienced variations on the scenario—we are just coping when something unforeseen and urgent crops up or someone falls sick. Having too much to do and not enough

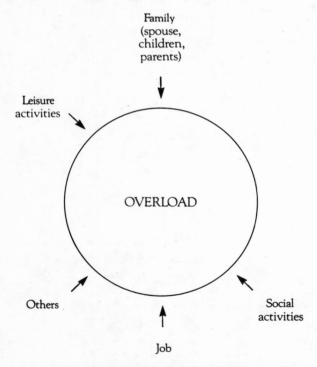

Fig 3   *Contributors to overload*

time in which to do it is a common problem and, put in such simple terms, the solution seems obvious. Either you need less to do, more time to do it in, or help to do it.

Why then, is sorting out the problem so difficult? Could it be that the demands on us are not straightforward after all? When we analyse what we have to do we rarely see the situation as a whole. Occasionally the problem may be contained and discrete, but usually a wide variety of other things intrude.

Often work overload is more than simply what happens in our job, but it is usually easier, and more comfortable, to see it as a 'work problem.'

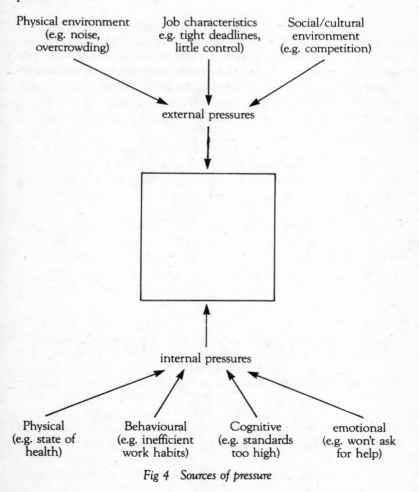

Fig 4   Sources of pressure

Demands are made on us from a variety of sources and contribute to a general feeling of pressure and overload (see Fig 3).

Sometimes demands may overlap and thus prevent otherwise simple solutions. If you could work late you could finish the new and urgent business but tonight your daughter's school concert, in which she has a starring role, is being held. How can you miss that? Thus it is not just a case of having too much to do, but of conflict between tasks and priorities.

This model of overload only considers external sources of demands but many pressures come from within ourselves, and it is these we see last. Figure 4 begins to explore in more detail the sources of pressure which lead to excessive demands.

One of the most difficult things to learn to do is to assess the pressures on yourself realistically. Most people have a tendency to see the pressures as either coming mainly from outside themselves, or being all to do with them. Moving to a more reasonable position requires hard work, perseverance, and an understanding of where demands really come from. It is only infrequently that we stop to consider physical pressures, for example, be it our own state of health or the physical environment of the work place.

Sometimes deciding where pressure originates will be difficult, particularly in the internal group. How you feel and think will interact with how you behave and it may not always be possible to sort out which came first. What is important is to see these three strands contributing to the pressures on you.

Many of the internal contributors to pressure have been discussed in the preceding chapters and others will appear later: for example, why you find managing your time difficult, problems with decision-making, and relationships with others at work. In this chapter we will concentrate on the external factors which contribute to demands at work.

THE PHYSICAL ENVIRONMENT

When the physical environment is mentioned in terms of job stress most people will immediately think of heavy industry, outdoor jobs, or occupations where someone has to go into dangerous situations. We rarely associate physical stresses with office work but there can be 'hidden' physical sources of pressure here, particularly in open-plan offices.

There is not space to consider all the specific physical stresses associated with various occupations but we can look at a few common problems.

Noise

Advances in engineering and technology have, in most cases, brought with them an increase in noise levels. The sound of typewriters, word processor keyboards and printers, photocopying machines, telephones and the general buzz of people talking and moving about can add up to considerable background noise in an open-plan office, especially if this is superimposed on muffled traffic sounds, workmen outside and sounds from the office next door.

Noise affects us in two ways. Firstly, it can damage hearing, ranging from deafness and temporary deafness (numbing over a period of time) to severely reduced sensitivity to certain sound frequencies. Secondly, a more generalized stress response includes mood changes and swings, impaired motor and intellectual functioning and changes in general behaviour and physical state.

An obvious point, but one frequently overlooked, is that noise interferes with communication between people, and speaking on the telephone is very easily disrupted. Noise can thus also produce hoarseness, coughs, throat lesions and pain if people have to strain to make themselves heard in constantly very noisy surroundings. In some circumstances noise might be important in the causing of accidents. For noise to be perceived and noted as a source of stress it usually has to be unwanted, irrelevant, abrupt, objectionable and disturbing.

The effect of noise on task performance is variable. It does not necessarily decrease performance; this depends in part on the duration and intensity of the noise and in part on the type of work involved. Tasks requiring both skill and speed or a high level of perceptual capacity will be affected most. Personality type is also involved. Anxious people are likely to be more at risk from the effects of noise.

Changing noise levels at work can be difficult and sometimes impossible. Where noise is part of the process or task, then some form of protection for your ears may be the only solution, but it is one that is easy and relatively cheap to implement. Cutting down noise in, for example, open-plan offices may be more difficult. Carpets or insulated vinyl flooring can absorb some noise, as can heavy curtains. Insulated screens between desks or work stations can improve matters, as can resiting equipment such as photocopiers and placing screens around them. These tend to be solutions which have to be taken up through staff committees or trade unions but there may be things you can do as well. Do you, for example, complain of noise from outside your office, but work with the door open?

Lighting

Lighting clearly needs to be appropriate for the task in hand but poor lighting is more likely to lead to people feeling gloomy, lethargic or generally fed-up than it is to major eye problems. Headaches can also occur, and are associated with frowning and screwing up your eyes in an attempt to see better.

Working in environments where there is no natural light often leads to low energy and morale. Some people are aware of feeling shut in, others do not realize they miss windows to look out of until they change to an office which has them. A building, or wall of a building, which is windowless can look oppressive as you approach it, giving the impression you are walking into a prison.

Full-spectrum fluorescent lighting in windowless offices may improve matters for those people who react poorly to the absence of ultra-violet light. Such people may not be aware that this was a problem; they just know that they feel better once the fluorescent light is installed. For those people who simply miss windows and 'outside', taking a walk at lunch-time or going to a room with a view outside for tea breaks is probably the easiest solution.

Air pollution

Major air pollution from any process you are engaged in is an area which should be covered by regulations on health and safety at work. Adequate ventilation, circulation of fresh air and filtration of stale, polluted air will again usually be issues to be taken up through unions or committees, especially in buildings with central facilities and sealed windows.

An increasingly common issue, however, seems more personal, at least on the surface, and that is smoking and working in a smoke-filled atmosphere. Smokers demand the freedom to smoke as part of their civil rights but, by the same token, non-smokers should have the right to a smoke-free atmosphere. Headaches, sore or watery eyes, and sore throats are the superficial effects of being in a smoky atmosphere. As more research reveals the very serious negative effects of passive smoking, the lobby for the right to a smoke-free work environment will surely increase.

Companies may impose policies banning smoking except in designated areas. If such rules are to be followed consistently then this means removing ashtrays as well as putting up 'no smoking' signs. It may be possible to segregate offices into smoking and non-smoking zones but logistics may make this less easy than it seems at first. If nothing else, good vertical ventilation should be installed to remove the pollution.

JOB CHARACTERISTICS

Some occupations by their very nature are more stressful than others. There is a tendency to think of occupational stress as applying mainly to the busy executive but such people often experience less stress than those in the ranks immediately below them. Part of the reason for this is attributable to having control over your working life—being rushed, but able to make decisions and to choose between one priority and another—is better than not being able to exert any control over what you have to do.

Interacting with job characteristics are personal factors, such as job satisfaction and what can be called 'job fit'—the square peg in a square hole (see pages 125-134). Intrinsic to that will be the ability to do the job.

Making generalizations about occupations is not very helpful. For example, clergymen are usually reported as registering high on job satisfaction scales and low on stress scales. This does not help the highly stressed inner-city clergyman who cannot cope with the overwhelming problems of his parishioners, or the clergyman unable to come to terms with his rural parish, having spent all his life in cities. That increasing numbers of the clergy are suffering from burnout, seeking divorce and leaving the ministry indicates that the picture of job stress is nothing like as straightforward as it is often presented.

Repetitive jobs

There is little that is as stressful in occupational terms as assembly-line working: working at repetitive, monotonous tasks at a fixed pace (to which *you* have to adjust, not it to you). The shorter the cycle of work, the more stress is experienced. Thus workers on assembly-line tasks lasting less than one minute experience more depression, gastro-intestinal disorders and disrupted sleep patterns than those on cycles of three minutes and over. Associated with assembly-line, machine-paced work are restrictive space requirements and noise levels which frequently cause the worker to be isolated from workmates.

The 'turning off' or 'tuning out' mechanisms which people employ to cope with boredom lead to feelings of alienation, including alienation from themselves. The mindless repetitiveness of some tasks can lead to errors being made which the operator is totally unaware of.

Various methods have been tried to reduce these stressful effects, including job rotation and job enlargement. The former involves workers rotating around jobs, either on a voluntary or obligatory basis. Although job satisfaction may be improved, it requires increased organization, disrupts social relationships, and may affect take-home pay as the worker has to re-adjust to new tasks.

Job enlargement involves combining two or more jobs, either of the same level (horizontal job enlargement) or across levels (vertical job enlargement), into one job. The latter usually means the worker takes on the tasks and responsibilities of the job immediately above him. Job satisfaction is improved, with all its attendant benefits. The logical extension of this is autonomous work groups which are responsible for producing the completed product. Such teams increase the worker's involvement and job satisfaction but are not without their own problems. They are usually more expensive in costs and time than line assembly, training requirements usually increase, and new and different social groups and leaders emerge.

Shift work

The stresses of shift work are of a very special kind. The body has very clear-cut, built-in daily rhythms, and these are disrupted by shift work. The body does make adjustments to working nights and sleeping days, for example, and this is why people on permanent night shift experience less stress than those whose work cycle varies every few weeks. The social problems associated with working very early, late or night shifts, however, can bring with them pressures of another kind. Some shift workers, such as nightwatchmen, also feel isolated from the rest of the workforce.

Travel and jet-lag

Jet-lag is analogous in many ways to shift work. The body's circadian rhythm is disrupted, leaving the individual disorientated and ill-equipped to deal with the tasks before him—and not just intellectual tasks. If your body thinks it is the early hours of the morning its ability to digest food will be poorer and it will be ill-equipped to deal with the meal being foisted on it because you are now on the west coast of America where it is evening. Many travellers on short-term business trips find the best way to cope with such stresses is to stay on *home* time for the duration. The more time zones crossed in any one trip, the more stress put on the individual.

The amount of foreign travel expected of many business people and politicians is excessive. For example, in the three months before his stroke Anthony Crosland, the British Foreign Secretary, made eleven trips to Europe.

Driving

In some cases driving *is* the job if you work as a chauffeur, taxi driver, deliveryman or long-distance lorry driver. In other professions it is not the work itself, but the means of carrying it out (if you are a salesman, for example). Business people may find themselves driving about the country, visiting clients, associates and colleagues; doctors, social workers and clergymen may have to drive round and round a small area making 'home visits'; and police-car drivers patrol their patch.

Although some people claim that driving helps them relax and unwind, it has to be said that driving is a stressful activity, particularly for men. Women's reactions to driving seem less drastic. Physical signs of stress are shown by drivers, even when they do not report feeling stress: heart-rate increases and there are increased levels of catecholamines excreted in urine.

The stress involved in driving derives from a number of factors, including traffic, weather and road conditions, navigating and getting lost, trouble with the car, general noise and vibration, fatigue and problems with passengers. Also, many people seem to undergo a profound personality change when driving. We do not need some strange elixir from Dr Jekyll to produce Mr Hyde—simply put him behind a steering wheel! One explanation for this behaviour hinges on the relative isolation of the driver from other people. The car forms an insulating box protecting the driver from face-to-face confrontations with other people. If you are alone there is no one to censure your anger. This anger is almost always directed at other drivers, and their behaviour can be taken as a personal insult, whether they are going too slow, in your opinion, or overtaking you recklessly. Some groups of people may arouse your emotions almost without doing anything, for example, women drivers or young people driving a newer, more powerful care than yours.

Passengers also contribute to stress by distracting the driver with their 'back-seat driving', poor navigating, unwarranted anxiety and the like. Children in particular can be a source of tension and distraction. Add muscle fatigue caused by sitting in a usually incorrect position for hours at a time and we see why driving can be stressful.

To make driving easier posture is important. You should not, either through positioning of the seat or muscle tension, be hunched over the steering wheel with your shoulders up around your ears and your neck and head jutting forward. If you clench your teeth and tense your jaw and neck muscles you may need to learn, away from the car, a specific relaxation technique to deal with this before you can put it into practice driving. Hands should rest on the steering wheel rather than grip it tightly. On a long-distance drive it is important to take adequate breaks. Three hours is probably long enough for anyone to drive without stopping. Regular brief halts are better than one longer one. Eating something, getting fresh air, stretching not only your legs but arms, shoulders and back, and going to the lavatory are all important aspects of the break and will help maintain alertness and concentration when you resume driving. Driving when you are tired is not only silly but dangerous, and driving and drinking can be both murderous and suicidal as well as being illegal. If you have to drive when you are tired, go a little more slowly than you would normally. When you begin to feel that every other driver on the road is behaving like an idiot it is more likely that your perception is at fault, due in part to tiredness.

Lastly, keep passengers, particularly children, under control. It is never too early to teach them never to distract the driver and games and other activities will help keep them quiet in the back seat. If a passenger is making driving impossible then you should stop and say so, and try to deal with the problem.

Other activities while you are in motion, particularly those which involve driving with only one hand on the wheel (such as using a phone), are also likely to be dangerous and slow down reactions in an emergency.

THE TYPE A ENVIRONMENT

Working in a Type A environment is a combination of job characteristics, role demands and, quite possibly, physical surroundings as well. Determining what is a real demand and what is a self-imposed one is a difficult exercise, but one of the most important to learn in managing stress.

Some occupations, as we have already discussed, encourage Type A behaviour in certain of their employees. Such pressures may be particularly difficult to resist if you have Type A tendencies anyway.

A Type A environment or job is one which expects everything and more—all the time. This is not the same as sudden crises or emergencies when you may have to work longer hours for a while, but a job which seems to demand permanent long hours, total involvement and little time for outside interests, including your family. Working to tight deadlines with more work coming in than you can handle also contributes to the stress-loading.

Decision making is an important aspect contributing to a Type A environment. Having to think quickly and make instant decisions, particularly where the wrong one will have disastrous consequences, is very stress-inducing, so is the unexpected. Lots of shocks, surprises, emergencies and not knowing what might happen next, allied to little prior planning (even where you *cannot* realistically plan ahead) will contribute to tension.

III
Coping with stress—
strategies and skills

6
Ineffective ways
of coping

Managing stress is more than just coping, it is learning to cope adaptively, effectively. It is nearly as important to know what not to do as what to try. Many people's first response to stress would be to light a cigarette or reach for a drink. These are ineffective ways of coping which, in the long run, do nothing to solve the cause of the stress and only add further problems.

SMOKING

There can be hardly a person in the country who is not aware of the dangers involved in smoking. Although smoking is decreasing among men it is rising among women, teenagers and children. Indeed the age of onset is getting younger and younger. Although it may bring a superficial sense of relief and calmness, it in fact sets off its own stress reaction by introducing nicotine into the blood stream. Tars and resins are carried to the lungs, decreasing their efficiency. As a result of smoking both adrenalin and noradrenalin are released, thus compounding the physical effects on the body.

As stress increases so does smoking. Giving up smoking is the only sensible thing to do, but this is not always easy. If smoking is closely tied to a stress reaction then learning to deal with the stress in a more adaptive way may make giving up smoking easier if you take it as a second step.

Some people smoke when they are bored as something to do to pass the time, or as a way of introducing something pleasurable and stimulating into the situation. Dealing with the root cause of the boredom or doing something which is less likely to kill you are better ways of handling the problem.

Many people would be horrified at the idea of taking drugs to manage stress; nevertheless they happily light up a cigarette. It should be borne in mind that nicotine itself is a powerful and very fast-acting drug.

ALCOHOL

Alcohol is also a powerful and fast-acting drug, widely used because of its effect on mood. It is hard to deny that used in relatively small amounts alcohol can have obvious value for the individual. It quickly produces feelings of well-being and satisfaction before, in larger doses, it moves on to produce euphoria and the release of social inhibitions. For many people this makes social interaction easier. Following on are garrulousness and recklessness, slurred speech, lack of co-ordination, impaired judgement and slowed reaction time. Beyond this a person is obviously drunk—first drunk and mobile, then drunk and stuporous, next dead drunk, being anaesthetized and comotose and, finally, simply dead.

Three factors: sex, weight and speed of drinking, all affect your blood alcohol concentration. Alcohol affects your judgement, so impairs not only driving, but also operating machinery and making decisions. You are more likely to take risks when you have been drinking, and this can interfere with your work on a number of levels.

Dependence on alcohol can be both physical and psychological. You may believe that you only drink a small amount and that you have no physical dependence, but if you feel that you *have* to have a drink when you get home from work before you can begin to unwind or the whole ritual of pouring a drink and sitting down with it is your cue to relax then maybe you have some sort of psychological dependency.

If you have a serious drink problem or are physically dependent on alcohol, then you will need professional help to deal with the problem. There are many options open and you should see your general practitioner in the first instance. If, however, your problem is less serious, but you are still worried about the amount you are drinking or believe that your drinking is getting out of hand, then there are a number of self-help options available (see Useful addresses, page 139). As with smoking, sorting out the root cause of stress or other problems may make dealing with drinking easier.

DRUGS

The use of legal or illegal drugs, including alcohol has increased dramatically in our society over the last 20 years. Taking drugs, even under medical supervision, is not usually the best way of dealing with stress since it does nothing to solve the problem behind it.

The most common drugs prescribed by GPs for stress and allied problems will be the minor tranquillizers and anti-depressants, including diazepam (Valium), chlordiazepoxide (Librium) and clorazepak (Tranxene) to calm you down during the day and nitrazepam (Mogadon) at night. As well as failing to solve the problem, tranquillizers can decrease the individual's ability to cope. Behaviourally, they can cause drowsiness, dull sensitivities and, with prolonged use, lessen intellectual capabilities. Also, because a person feels less stressed he may not be so motivated to deal with the problem; possibly, taking the drug may become a positive, rewarding action in its own right. At this point the individual is on the way to psychological and, according to which drug is taken, physical dependence.

If you are taking tranquillizers and want to stop, consult with your GP first. If he/she is unhelpful then consult one of the organizations listed on page 139.

DIET AND EATING

What you eat can be contributory to certain illnesses; for example, a diet high in animal fats seems to be linked with coronary heart disease. Where stress is concerned, a balanced healthy diet is important if you are to maintain a healthy body which can withstand it, but it is rather the behavioural aspects of eating which are likely to be affected. Some people eat less or almost stop eating under stress; others eat more, reaching out for their own particular 'comfort food'.

Both groups need to be aware of their problem and take steps to overcome it. If your difficulty is not wanting to eat, and this feeling lasts more than a day or two, then try to eat as you would if you were feeling unwell or recovering from flu. Light, easily digested food and small servings will usually help, as will 'a little of what you fancy' rather than forcing yourself to eat big, heavy meals which you do not want. Plenty of fresh fruit and vegetables are usually acceptable—and healthy.

If you reached for fresh fruit and vegetables when tempted to eat by stress you would not really have a problem. The problem arises because you are more likely to crave something high in either sugar or fat or both. You know whether it is a real problem for you or not. If it causes you to be overweight then it is a problem. If it is only an occasional habit it might not matter so much. Nevertheless, you can improve the habit. Wholemeal bread is better than a sugary Danish pastry if you must have carbohydrate or stodge, but fruit would be better still. Sugary canned drinks rot your teeth as well as expanding your waistline, and there are hazards associated with elevating your blood sugar level quickly in this way. Excessive coffee is not a good idea either. Change to fruit juice or mineral water.

Being under stress can also cause you to miss meals, eat on the move, or bolt your food. An occasional missed meal is not going to hurt anyone, but if you become irritable and impatient as a result of lowered blood sugar, your judgement may be less acute. Eating on the move and bolting your food may lead to indigestion. Although not in itself serious, coupled with other symptoms of stress it is likely to impair your efficiency. The answer is to return to the habits you learnt as a child—or are currently trying to instil in your own children! Sit down to eat, preferably at a table, eat slowly, chew your food and do not speak with your mouth full. Putting your knife and fork down as you chew your food rather than immediately reloading is possibly the easiest way of slowing yourself down. None of this need take very long, but 10 minutes at your desk eating your sandwich is much better than driving with one hand and eating with the other. You are less likely to spill it down you, as well!

OVERWORK

You are more likely to consider overwork the cause of your stress than a way of coping, but many people try to cope with the problems by working longer and longer hours. 'If only I could catch up,' they believe, 'everything would be all right.' But it rarely is, because they are not looking at what is causing the extra work in the first place. We have touched on many of these causes already—poor time management, too-high standards or too many extrinsic tasks.

Working for too long a time, without adequate rests or change, is likely to cause errors to increase and lead you to become otherwise inefficient—generating yet more work.

Lastly, overwork can be a way of masking other problems. You may be overworked because you are generally inefficient or because you do not have the necessary competence or skills to do the job. Then again, you may have problems with your family and staying at work is better than going home to face them. Either way, dealing with these problems will stop the need for overwork—if it is overwork you have labelled as a problem. Even if you have not, overwork will not deal with the real issues.

7
Staying healthy

The role of good physical health, including the importance of a balanced healthy diet, in aiding the individual to overcome stress has already been outlined. There are a number of other areas that contribute to staying healthy and combating stress that can be grouped together here.

EXERCISE

It is said that there is one exercise to suit each person and which that person will enjoy. People who exercise believe this; those who don't, don't. The exercise story is a combination of good news and bad news—much depends on *why* you exercise. There is no doubt that exercise contributes to cardiovascular fitness; that is, your heart copes more effectively and efficiently with the everyday demands placed on it. There is no substantial proof, however, that exercise reduces the risk of having a coronary or lengthens your life, and there *is* evidence of exercise killing people—or maybe it is fairer to say of people dying suddenly at a time of strenuous activity. When books and magazines suggest that you check with a doctor before taking up exercise they mean it. It stops you—or your next of kin—being able to sue them, should an accident happen. An examination will not necessarily tell you that you are fit to exercise. All it can tell you is that you definitely should not, for example, if you have uncontrolled high blood pressure, angina, or are very overweight.

Having said all this, exercise does bring benefits. People claim they feel fitter and healthier and it *does* improve your cardiovascular system and use of lungs; it is an inefficient way of trying to lose weight but can improve shape and muscle tone. Seeing yourself shape up, or simply having the self-discipline to keep to a regular exercise regime can all improve psychological well-being. And no one should under-estimate the effects of distraction. It is almost impossible to worry and jog!

I have already mentioned the particular problem that many Type As have in exercising and that is being overly competitive. Exercising in a group or as part of a team will tend to contribute to a competitive atmosphere. Exercising alone may overcome this.

The amount of exercise you need to become and keep fit is almost certainly less than the evangelists claim. Pulse rate is one guide, and is a good way of gauging 'improvement', but it is easy to over-estimate your fitness in this way. For most people, the best and simplest guide is not to exercise to the point where you cannot talk comfortably to someone with you. And if that means after walking up a couple of flights of stairs then you know it is time to start taking exercise — gently.

Never keep on exercising if you have even the slightest chest pain, or if you start to feel dizzy, lightheaded, overcome by fatigue or otherwise distressed. You want to be fit enough to enjoy life, not to be a healthy corpse.

SLEEP

Persistent sleep problems can be debilitating but worry over not sleeping can be even more so. Keep a diary over a two-week period to record how much sleep you are getting and how you feel the next day. If you spend long periods awake in bed before falling asleep yet you feel fine the next day, reconsider whether you are one of those people who do not need eight hours' sleep. Research has shown that many people need less. If you habitually sleep for nine to ten hours or more and still feel tired, and your doctor tells you you are healthy, try sleeping fewer hours for a while. Too much sleep can leave you feeling tired, lethargic and apathetic.

If you have difficulty sleeping only use sleeping tablets as a last resort. Try behavioural methods first. These vary, and are sometimes contradictory—find which suits you.

- Only go to bed when you are tired, not by the clock.
- Go to bed and get up at set, rigid times. This will train you to sleep during those times.
- Get up an hour earlier—this may take discipline, but you should find you feel tired earlier.
- Take more exercise.
- Do not eat a full meal just before going to bed.
- Do not take stimulants before going to bed—this includes alcohol, tea, coffee, and soft drinks containing caffeine.

- Go to bed to sleep, not to read or to sit propped up and work.
- Try a warm bath before going to bed.
- Make sure you are comfortable and warm in bed.
- Is background noise disturbing you? Try moving your bed, sleeping in a different room, or buy earplugs.

Although some people, for whom getting to sleep is difficult, find relaxation a useful way of calming down and inducing sleep, that is not its main purpose; methods of relaxation will be discussed in the next section.

RELAXATION

Early on in this book I said that coping with stress involved learning new skills. Relaxing is a skill. It may not solve your stress problem by itself, but it may put you in a state where you are able to think about or reflect on a problem. It may also deal with a number of aches and pains caused by tension.

For relaxation to 'work', that is, to bring down your blood pressure, you have to give it a fair try and believe in it. If you want to prove it is rubbish you can—for yourself at least. If you are at all sceptical then learning to relax from a book, record or tape is going to be difficult. And by relaxing I do not mean sitting with your feet up reading a good book—and certainly not watching the football on TV! Most forms of relaxation owe something to Jacobsen who developed a procedure for progressive muscle relaxation in the 1920s and 1930s. Groups of muscles are alternately tensed and relaxed, until the whole body is relaxed. Briefly, the sequence involves tensing, then letting go:

1. The muscles in the right hand and forearm—make a fist
2. The muscles in the upper right arm—push your elbow down against the chair arm
3. The muscles of the left hand and forearm
4. The muscles of the left upper arm
5. The muscles in the upper part of the face—lift your eyebrows as high as you can
6. The muscles in the central part of the face—squint your eyes or screw them up, at the same time wrinkling your nose
7. The muscles in the lower part of your face—bite your teeth together, clench your jaw at the same time pulling the corners of your mouth back

8. The muscles of the neck—pull your chin down towards your chest, at the same time working to prevent it touching your chest
9. The muscles of the chest, shoulder and upper back—take a deep breath and while doing this pull your shoulder blades together
10. The muscles of the abdomen—make your stomach hard, either by pulling it in or pushing it out
11. The buttocks—pull them together
12. The muscles of the right thigh—counterpose the large muscle on top with the two smaller at the back
13. The muscles of the lower right leg and foot—stretch your leg pointing your toes towards the floor
14. The muscles of the left thigh
15. The muscles of the left lower leg and foot.

These can be combined:

- 1 and 2—hold your arm in front of you with your elbow bent and make a fist
- 3 and 4
- 5, 6 and 7
- 8
- 9, 10 and 11
- 12 and 13—lift your leg off the chair slightly, point your toes and, at the same time, turn your foot inward

After practice, combine the muscle groups thus:

- 1, 2, 3 and 4
- 5, 6, 7 and 8
- 9, 10 and 11
- 12, 13, 14 and 15

Some other techniques place greater emphasis on breathing, and controlling rate and speed of breathing.

Whatever relaxation technique you choose you should be aware the people who need to relax the most are those least likely to persevere in learning. If you want to release tension and relax in moments of stress then you need to learn the skill over time, practising regularly. It is not just a 'little trick' you can pick up in half an hour. Like learning anything else you have to use a certain amount of discipline to acquire the technique in the first place. Going to a class often helps.

There are a number of other techniques or disciplines which have something to do with managing physical tension but which offer more than just relaxation, and some will be mentioned briefly.

Biofeedback

Although biofeedback showed a lot of clinical promise during the 1970s this has not really been fulfilled. True, individuals attached to a biofeedback machine showed impressive drops in blood pressure but this was not generally passed on to everyday life. Most people need something they can check internally to gauge their responses in an ordinary setting. It might be possible to learn this through biofeedback but professional help is generally needed—if only to provide the machine.

The Alexander Technique

The Alexander Technique is much more than merely a way of reducing physical tension. It is difficult to explain exactly what it is—it needs to be experienced. Among other things it is a way of finding, learning or re-establishing better body habits, including posture, and making better use of feedback from your own body. People with stiff necks, a bad back, general aches and pains and tension headaches usually benefit quickly. Anyone who suffers aches and pains because of their job and the things it requires them to do—be it a violinist sitting slightly askew, a nurse required to lift heavy patients, or a keyboard operator with an aching neck and shoulders—will benefit from the technique, developing better habits in the use of the body. One advantage of the Alexander Technique is that if you are going to benefit then you will know this quickly. A disadvantage is that it cannot be learnt from a book; you have to have hands-on experience with a teacher.

Massage

Massage can be an excellent aid to relaxation. The neck and feet are the areas of the body which benefit most. Although it is possible to massage your own feet someone else really needs to do your neck and back. It is worth having a professional massage at least once to know what it feels like, even if most of the time you rely on a friend or relative.

Yoga

Yoga spans both relaxation and our next category, meditation. Yoga is a centuries-old Hindu tradition, but many people derive immense benefit from its system of relaxation without believing in its religious foundations. Although it is possible to learn yoga from a book, it is better and easier to learn yoga from classes. Having achieved a fairly deep level of relaxation you can stop there and enjoy this, or move on to the next stage—meditation.

Meditation

The hype that surrounded transcendental meditation, its promise of cure for many psychological and physical problems and illnesses has put many people off the whole idea. Yet meditation can be a very useful technique in helping control restlessness, anxiety, inability to concentrate or fragmented thinking and tension. To practise meditation you need have no particular religious or spiritual beliefs, nor need you be steeped in the philosophy of the East. Many people practise meditation within a Christian belief system or indeed within an entirely secular framework.

There is a number of varieties and finding the one that suits you is important. You may prefer to learn from a teacher or to teach yourself. You need to know you will not be disturbed (for, say 20 minutes) and to be comfortable (posture and temperature). Most people find it easiest to close their eyes and practise relaxation first, and then allow their thoughts to quieten by dwelling on an object, symbol, word or the rhythm of their breathing. In transcendental meditation each student is given a personal mantra (sacred word) by their teacher during initiation and must promise never to reveal it. Although some people like using Sanskrit words or phrases you can find your own to repeat. The ancient Siddha Yoga mantra *Om Namah Shivaya*, or its first word 'Om', is popular, but words such as 'one', 'relax' or 'peace' are equally effective. Some people prefer a single syllable such as 'peace', as it is easier to chant.

As with relaxation, persistence is necessary both to master the technique and derive benefit. Gradually, distracting thoughts will occur less often and it will be easier to maintain a passive attitude and to take a step back to watch yourself.

As well as keeping lower blood pressure whilst you are actually meditating, this exercise can provide a much-needed break in a hectic schedule, give you time to distance yourself from problems, help you delay, if not always avoid, panic and give you a basis of calm from which to proceed into the day.

SPIRITUAL BELIEFS

For many people meditation and their spiritual beliefs go hand in hand, and they may combine them with activities such as prayer. Whilst no one can develop a belief system on demand, and to try to do so simply to combat stress would almost surely lead to failure, there is some evidence that belief in *something* is important in maintaining psychological health. Such beliefs are not necessarily religious, but offer the individual a way of viewing the world and his place in it, usually in a way which offers both acceptance and challenge, hope and a sense of the realistic. A phrase which sums up your belief may be helpful in some stress situations—at least some of the time, 'what will be, will be' may be important. More useful is the traditional prayer, 'Lord, grant me the strength to change that which needs changing, the courage to accept that which cannot be changed, and the wisdom to know the difference.'

PLAY

As we grow older many of us forget how to play, or even how to use our leisure time for our own benefit. We find it taken up with chores and the overspill from our paid work. Play enables children to let off steam, and provides diversions and distractions, freedom and room for self-expression. Children also learn through play.

Put like that, how can any adult afford not to play? Some form of recreation is necessary for all of us. It should be enjoyable, affordable (!), provide us with change and allow us to express ourselves. But not necessarily all the time. To expect all your leisure time to be challenging, creative or meaningful is to expect too much, and to set yourself impossible, stressful goals. Everyone at some stage should collapse in front of a soap opera, sports game or children's programme—and really enjoy it, with a clear conscience.

Whatever your chosen method of recreation it should not become so serious that it becomes another stressor. It is as well to bear in mind that laughter is a great releaser of tension, and one approved of by society, available any time, anywhere, and free. Learn to laugh honestly at yourself and half your battle with stress is won.

8
General principles of coping and changing

Before coming on to more specific ways of dealing with particular stressors, we should consider some general rules and guidelines for promoting change and coping. An understanding of the basic principles means that you can devise your own solutions to problems as they arise.

CHANGE

In managing stress there are usually three areas in which change can be effected: namely, yourself, others, and the environment. Sometimes one will be the clear target but if it proves difficult to do anything about that then you may need to move to another area.

Wanting others or the environment to change is not the same thing as it actually happening. It may suit other people to stay as they are and if your boss is one of these, your chances of directly influencing their behaviour may be slim.

At this point how much control you have in a situation will directly influence how you tackle problems. If you are in a position of authority you can insist on change (although this is not usually the best way of dealing with a difficulty). Stress is more likely to be encountered where you do not have much control, and devising ways to cope may stretch your inventiveness. Most stress or frustration is likely to arise in situations in which you are responsible or accountable, but have no real authority to decide how something is done or to implement change. When we consider analysing problems in the next section it should become clear that this is the real problem and probably needs to be dealt with at an organizational level.

You may believe that there is very little you can do about a situation because you have no control or authority. Sometimes this may be so but there are always possibilities—and acceptance, although indeed a possibility, is not always the answer.

As well as needing the right opportunity, implementing change also involves having the necessary skills and motivation to do it. The techniques that can be used both to promote change and to learn new skills overlap.

THE CONSEQUENCES OF ACTION

Part of learning is performance. We might know what we should, or could, do to improve our stress problems, we may even know how to do it, but somehow never get round to it. There could be a number of reasons for this, but very often it is because we fear the consequences of our actions. Maybe you believe that if you face your boss over the issue of an unrealistic work load requiring too much overtime you will end up having a row, losing your chance of promotion, being given an ultimatum—accept or quit, or being fired. We often leap to unnecessarily negative conclusions about the consequences of our actions. The first thing to consider is, How realistic are your expectations? Go back and reread the section on beliefs and attitudes, if necessary (pages 37-39).

If you decide that a negative outcome is possible, how serious is it? How big a risk are you prepared to take? This depends on factors such as your personality, how much stress the problem is causing you, personal and family situation and so forth. Most change involves some risk and often things get worse before they get better. If you are unwilling to face this you will be unlikely to want to face change. People in a rut, even a fairly miserable rut, can hold surprisingly fast to the status quo. Mumbling and grumbling, moaning and groaning are, in many instances, an inevitable part of the change process.

It should be obvious, at this point, that if change is seen to have positive results, both you and others will be more likely to implement it. It is not always possible to guarantee that the outcome will be exactly what you want, but you can improve the odds by being positive about certain aspects. The following sections on goal-setting and problem-solving will help you in devising alternative plans of action which are achievable and whose results are measurable.

Having done this, you can manipulate some of the consequences to ensure that you end up with something positive. We all do this without thinking much of the time—'When I've made this difficult phone call I'll have a coffee', 'If I get this report finished I'll knock off early', and so on. These are extrinsic rewards and if you are disciplined enough *not* to have the coffee until you have phoned and you *want* a coffee, this technique may work well for you. There are also intrinsic rewards, namely satisfaction at having something out of the way, and freedom from the anxiety of something unpleasant hanging over you.

The problem arises when what you do does not work out as you hoped. The phone call goes wrong and coffee seems a poor reward. The coffee was contingent on you *doing* something, however, not on the outcome. Be positive that you tackled something you found difficult—*then* go back and analyse why it went wrong and learn from this what to do next time. Remember the old school reports that had a column for effort and a column for achievement? Do not forget to give yourself stars for effort.

Even if, at the end of the day, you believe that only achievement counts, remember that here I am talking about *learning* new skills, *starting* to change—and these take effort. All the effort in the world does not guarantee you a positive outcome, which is why you need feedback to monitor progress, but very little is achieved without effort.

GOAL-SETTING

There is an art—or maybe it is a science—to goal-setting that makes attaining your desired aim easier and involves a number of simple guidelines. When setting goals many of us have a tendency to be vague and global. We want a lot to change.

What are your goals at the moment? To be less stressed? To feel less pressurized? One of the difficulties with objectives like these is how to know when you have reached them. It's like saying 'I want to be happy'—how will you know when you are? You might be happy but maybe you could be happier still. The answer is to set goals that are specific and measurable. 'I want to be rich' may sound more specific than 'I want to be happy,' but is it? As we approach our goal we often change it. To most people being a millionaire may indeed be owning riches, but as you come close to achieving this you may realize that you are not as rich as others are—so you set a new goal. If you had been specific—albeit £1,000,000 specific—you would know you had succeeded in reaching your first goal. If you had simply stated 'rich' you would never feel you had achieved anything. To meet the criteria of being both specific and measurable you should always ask yourself 'How will I know when I have achieved it?' If you cannot answer this, redraft your goal.

But this is only part of the story. Your goal may be 'I want to be chairman of ICI.' This is both specific and measurable. You, and everyone else, will know when you have reached it. But is it achievable? Setting realistic goals seems defeatist to some people—if you do not reach for the stars how will you get to the moon? They see it as limiting potential. The other side to this is that by setting goals which are unobtainable you are more likely to face frequent failure, which is depressing and demoralizing. The answer to this dilemma is straightforward—small steps. Break down your goal into as many small steps or tasks as it takes to make them achievable. This makes it clear what you have to do and whether you have to learn new skills, and at what stage. It means each step on the way can be enjoyed as a positive move forward rather than the experience turning into a constant frustrated longing for something still out of reach. You also gain more control over what you do and what you want to do and you have the freedom to accept new possibilities or see other directions in which you may choose to go. There is the option to stop wherever you want, for as long as you want, without feeling that everything is lost.

How you phrase your aim is also important. It is better to set positive goals than negative ones. Say 'I want to feel more relaxed' rather than 'I want to be less tense' or 'I want to enjoy my work more' rather than 'I want to be under less pressure.' You should then turn these into specific, measurable, achievable objectives but you may find this alters your perspective. You may well begin to think of things to add to the situation as well as take away. 'Not having so much to do' may mean you are under less pressure, but 'having a social lunch with colleagues' may bring positive enjoyment.

Managing stress means more than getting rid of what is unpleasant or 'stressful'; it also involves adding things which are positive and enjoyable. This is particularly important if you decide that there really is nothing to be done about a particular situation. Adding something positive may make it bearable.

PROBLEM-SOLVING SKILLS

Much of the time we do not notice that we are solving problems. We make everyday decisions as a matter of course—what to wear, what to eat, whether to go to the cinema or theatre. Often even big decisions such as whether to change jobs, move house, get married, get divorced are resolved without too much difficulty. The real difficulties come, not always because we do not know what to do, but because we do not like the decision we have reached. The reason for this may be because we cannot put it into effect (we do not have the skills or resources, or it is illegal or immoral) or because it does not give us what we wanted.

Solving a problem does not always guarantee that we get exactly what we want, but having a solution we *cannot* act on is no more helpful than having no solution. Maybe there are other answers but you have not seen them for various reasons. Learning problem-solving skills means following through a sequence of procedures rather than assuming your first idea has to be the only one. It is useful to write down your thoughts at each stage so that you do not lose track of them or forget anything.

Identify problems

First state your problem or problems. If there are several, list them in any order for the moment. It is often useful to restate a problem in several ways, so that you have several viewpoints or angles on it. If there are two or more of you involved in this exercise this is especially important. Knowing as much as you can about the problem is helpful in finding solutions. It is also worth digging beneath the surface of the problem to see if there is another more fundamental issue at stake. Consider your part in the problem. Do not simply say 'my boss' or 'overwork'. Be more precise and give examples. Does everyone find the boss difficult or only you? If so, why?

Giving real thought to the nature of the major problem is often overlooked. It is too easy to give a quick, superficial outline—and one that minimizes your role.

Identify priorities and goals

Having sorted out what the problems are you are now in a position to list your priorities. At this stage do not worry about how you are going to achieve your end; just list, in order, what it is you want. At this point you may find yourself going beyond merely listing problems you want to be rid of, but including other goals as well. The next section considers the art of setting goals in more detail.

Identifying priorities means balancing what is urgent but trivial and what is not urgent but important. We will return to this point in the chapter on time management (see page 91).

Identify solutions

Write down as many ways of dealing with the problem as you can think of. Do not discuss them, do not put them in order of merit, do not disregard any—all that will come later. Many people stop when they have one or two answers, assuming that there are no others, or that these must be best because they thought of them first. If you have trouble allowing your mind and imagination to run free, set a target of at least six different solutions and make one of them 'silly' or 'impossible'. If trouble with your boss or a subordinate is the problem, for example, one solution might be to kill the offending person. Now it is unlikely (I hope) that you would consider this a suitable solution—but it is a solution, and may open the way to wondering about other, more ethical, ways of removing someone, i.e. you could encourage your boss to seek promotion, or transfer a subordinate. Remember the three areas in which changes might happen: yourself, others, and the environment. Find answers in each of these. This technique is often known as 'brainstorming'—you write everything down uncritically. If you stop to discuss anything then your fund of ideas will quickly dry up. Never be satisfied with one solution; there are always alternatives.

Consider solutions

Only once you have a reasonable list of solutions should you begin to consider or discuss them. At this point some will be discarded as contravening the laws of man, God or nature; others will be seen as merely unattractive. Some discussion of practicality will inevitably occur but you should not fall into the trap of confusing a discussion of solutions with planning their implementation.

Preferred solution

Decide which solution best fits your priorities and goals.

Planning

It is only at this stage that you should begin planning your strategy for implementing your decision. This may involve considering options for carrying out your preferred solution, depending on how precisely you stated it.

It is more than likely that your solution will involve a number of steps and it is important to be aware, at this stage, of every detail and what skills you are likely to need. It may be that at this point a major flaw in your solution is discovered; you do not have the skills or resources to enact your plan and you may need to go back to considering solutions to find the next best one.

Getting reactions from other people is useful, so that you have several opinions on how things may go and you can plan to cover most eventualities. You will never be able to cover all possible situations but it is important to feel that you have the skills necessary to cope with whatever is most likely to happen. The confidence that comes from this will be invaluable when you put your plan into action.

Rehearsal

Depending on what you are doing, you may want to rehearse or run through parts of your plan. Practising what you are going to say is often useful, but not if you become so tied to a particular 'script' that you are totally thrown if someone responds differently to how you planned.

Rehearsing with someone else can be particularly helpful. In this sort of 'role-play' the person you are rehearsing with acts out the part of the person you are having difficulties with. If someone new to the problem comes in at this stage he may well bring a new dimension to it as well. In some cases this may result in having to go back to the beginning. For this reason some people like to role-play when analysing the problem. It can be enlightening to take the role of the person you will have to tackle and have the person helping you play your part. This can give you a much clearer insight into your own part in the problem. Again, this can be usefully done as a first step in analysing the problem.

Put your plan into operation

No more procrastination, planning or generally prevaricating. At this point you simply get on and do what you have planned and rehearsed.

Feedback

Go over the success or otherwise of your strategy. If it worked, reward yourself, and be sure you know why it worked. If it did not, discover why not. Where was your planning at fault? Was it in your analysis of the problem? Your lack of skill in implementing your strategy? Did you lose your temper when you did not intend to? What can you learn from what has happened to improve your analysis of a situation and the solutions you devise?

Repeat as necessary

If your solution was less than optimal you will need to go back to the 'Identify solutions' stage to find another idea. If you achieve your aim then you can go back to identifying priorities and goals to tackle the next on your list.

9
Managing time

We all know that time is inelastic, that we cannot store it and, although it is infinite itself, we only have a finite amount of it. Despite the persuasions of various science-fiction writers none of us truly believes we can go back in time, so all we can influence is the present and, through this, the future.

For many people, learning to manage their time better would solve most, if not all, of their stress problems. At first glance, managing time seems to mean being better organized, working faster or more efficiently and wasting less time. All it takes is a bit of discipline and organization. This is true to an extent, but more is involved than will-power and simple logistics. Many of us look for ways to save time in much the same way as we would save money. The difference is that money can be stored (and gathers interest)—time cannot be hoarded up in the same way. The odd hour we have free now cannot be put away and brought out in a few weeks when we are busy or added on to our holiday. The only way we have of 'saving' time is by making the best use of it as it comes along.

TIME DIARY

The first step in managing time, like managing money, is to know what you do with it; keeping a record of how you spend your time, like a record of how you spend your money, can bring some nasty surprises. It gives you an indication of where you are frittering time away and where you can make 'savings'. There are also some pleasant surprises. At some time most of us have said 'I do not know where the day/week went' or 'I don't seem to have accomplished anything today'. Your time diary can show you *exactly* where the week went, and that you have done more than you thought.

Begin keeping a time diary of your working life today. At first it will simply tell you what you are doing during the day, but over time it will record changes and improvements in your routine. There are three basic ways to record what you do.

- List times, e.g. every half-hour, and record what you are doing at that particular time. This will work if your job involves spending long periods of time at one task, or if you only want a crude estimate. For providing a real baseline and monitoring change it is not enough.

- List everything you do, with a start time and how long it takes. This is usually the best way to begin, otherwise tasks that only take a few minutes get lost. It is also useful in that it automatically monitors interruptions, changes of task and so on. It is impossible to fool yourself (as long as you have filled it in honestly) as to where your time is going or being wasted.

- You could choose to have a list of tasks that you habitually perform and simply log the amount of time you spend at each one, adding it up at the end of the day. One drawback with this is that you are unlikely to log the odd interruption which only takes five minutes or so, but which in a day add up to a considerable amount of time.

Developing the categories for the third option is a skill in itself, and is often easier if you have spent a week or so recording your activities as described in the first and second methods. They should neither be so wide as to be meaningless or so narrow that you end up with hundreds. If you do have too many categories, you are better sticking to the second option. Inevitably a miscellaneous category is needed; but care should be taken that you do not end up with a large amount of time accounted for here. If you do, your category system needs expanding.

You can either list activities, e.g. dealing with mail, attending meetings, making phone calls, writing reports, or list projects or accounts and include all the work, be it mail, phone calls, writing, etc. under each. For most people a combination of the two works well—although you should remember not to record something twice. If your category is too large, you may need to break it down to see where the time really goes.

The amount of detail depends on your own preference and how out of control you are. As a rough guide, the worse your problem with time management, the more information you need to regain control. Do not let recording take over, though.

Combining the second and third options is often the most appropriate at first. Although it looks complex and time-consuming you will not be doing it for ever and the results can be very useful. At the end of a day recording what you have done, tot up the amounts of time spent on a particular activity and enter the time total in the relevant category.

A last word on this to remind you to include *all* the time you spend working—this includes at home in the evenings and at weekends. If one of your goals is to establish a better balance between your work and personal life and to use your free time better, you could include your leisure activities in your time diary. This is particularly important for people whose job does not have clear demarcations, or who habitually work from home.

JOB DEMANDS

Why are you here?

This question is not asked in a philosophical or cosmic sense, but aims to establish what your tasks at work are. What is it your employers (and employees) expect of you? What is your job description?

If you do not have a job description, you are not alone; if you would not recognize yours if it landed on your desk, you have problems. As a start, use your time diary to list all your activities (List 1). Some of these will be major categories, others fairly minor, but they should account for *all* your time.

If you can find a job description, use this to make a list of tasks you should be doing (List 2). If a job description does not exist, write a list of what you would expect someone with your job title to do. If possible, discuss your job description with your boss and even those people who work under you. What do they expect of you?

Compare the two lists. How many tasks appear on List 1 and not on List 2? This gives you an rough estimate of how much time you spend on tasks which are outside the confines of your job. Before you eliminate these, however, carry out the following exercise.

First divide your tasks and activities into three categories: (1) things you *must* do, (2) things you *should* do and (3) things you *want* to do. For most people 'what must be done' will take up most time, but some jobs give much greater flexibility. Be ruthless. Must means *must*—it is your responsibility, the essential part of your job. These are tasks you cannot ignore, delegate or bungle. 'What you should do' contains tasks about which there is some option, either when or how they are done, or possibly whether they are delegated. 'What you want to do' should be obvious.

What tasks are now left on your original list which do not fit any of the above categories? Why are you doing them?

Where do demands come from?

The immediate answer is from your boss, but consider further. Does your boss delegate enough or too much? Are your subordinates too dependent on you? Do you delegate enough (or too much)? Do your peers or co-workers off-load any of their work on you? Look carefully at your list of tasks to see whether some of what you are doing appears on someone else's job description.

Having done this, consider the demands you make on yourself and the number of tasks you perform out of habit or because 'someone has to do it'. Are these jobs trivial or important? How long do they take? Even if a task only takes five minutes (many will take a lot longer), think of the pressure that comes from remembering that it has to be done and wondering how you are going to fit it in.

Take plants, for example. Many offices have plants—who cares for them? If it is part of someone's job to look after them, or contractors deal with it, fine. If it is your plant, that *you* want on your desk, fine. But if there is a number of plants, scattered about, that have 'appeared' and you feel you must water them, that is a different story. Wandering round, feeding and watering a couple of dozen plants, picking off dead leaves and generally fussing over them eats into a crowded timetable. It only adds to your work load—particularly if you worry when they are not doing well! If, however, you ignore them until you have *time*, and then if you use the task positively to unwind, the same activity can have very different consequences.

Watering plants may seem trivial, but apply the same principle to all the 'housekeeping' or general 'clearing up' tasks you do because no one else does them, and the time begins to mount up. I would include in this category organizing office social events, such as the Christmas party, inter-office tournaments, and so on. If they *have* to be done, make sure they rotate!

PRIORITIES

Setting priorities is a skill, and one well worth learning. Although it includes yet more lists, it is considerably more than simply a list of things to do. From your lists of tasks—what must be done, what should be done and what you would like to be done—you can begin to sort out the major tasks from the minor ones, urgent and non-urgent, and long-term goals from short-term goals.

How you spend your time should also be classified into tasks which are active or initiating, and those which are reactive or are a response to what is going on around you. A common problem in managing time is to find that so long is spent on responding and reacting to daily events that you never have time to deal with the initiating parts of your job, which are usually more important and enjoyable.

Active tasks are those which help you gain your own objectives and those of the organization for which you work. They may be short- or long-term goals, and should include your own personal development.

Two other things must be established—how important the task is and how urgent it is. To a large extent, importance determines the length of time you spend on a task. Many things we do out of habit. Do you have to attend *all* the meetings you go to? Ask yourself what purpose is being served.

The trick is creating a balance between all these factors. Urgent tasks are not necessarily important and should be dealt with straight away, in minimum time. If, however, you spend all your time reacting to trivial, urgent tasks, you never have time for the longer-term, important tasks. A big report, which has to be ready in a month or a week, is put off in favour of more urgent matters until time runs out and the report is urgent, too. At this point you give it top priority, but also know that you no longer have time to do the really good job you had planned.

So setting priorities involves forward planning—for both long-term goals and today's. It helps to break long-term or complex goals down into a series of small, achievable tasks (see chapter 8) and incorporate these into your schedule.

Once a plan has been drawn up, the real secret of time management is to carry it through. To do this may involve moving into other areas, such as delegation and dealing with interruptions, emergencies and the like.

Forward planning

Forward planning does not mean being so organized that every second is accounted for, or so rigid that you cannot act on a sudden opportunity or even a whim. It does not mean the end of spontaneity and a sense of fun and challenge. It does mean the end of wondering how and when you are going to do everything and feeling too frazzled to enjoy it.

It does not mean knowing what you are doing in six months' time in detail—but it does mean not being caught out by snow in winter, or the annual conference 'suddenly' only being a month away.

The past couple of years have seen a boom in the trend for organizer diaries, but whether you choose an expensive leather-bound version, one of the complex organizer systems or make do with a notebook or the company-provided diary, you need something to write in. How you end up organizing this depends on your personal style, inventiveness and type of job you are involved in.

Basically you should have a long-term goal list, covering six months or more, which outlines future events and tasks, many of which will require some work currently. Deadlines can be written in—for conferences, trips, reports and so on—but the tasks that you need to complete for these matters will be planned, in small stages, in other lists.

Then you should draw up a medium-term list to carry you over the next month, a short-term list of what has to be done this week, and your daily list. Once you have such a system underway it takes very little time to organize; you can stop worrying that something is being forgotten or neglected, and you can derive enormous satisfaction from crossing things off each list.

Your 'to do' list includes writing or phoning others, planning, preparation, meetings, dealing with mail and so on. It is often worth noting personal chores to be performed during the day as well. This eliminates both the panic you usually feel when you try to remember what it was you had to do, knowing it was important, and the frustration of remembering five minutes after the shop shuts.

Wall charts and planners can serve as your record of deadlines and long-term goals, are visible and thus can be motivating, but also lack privacy. The inevitable coloured pins, stickers and so on can provide endless excuses for re-organizing the system . . . and wasting time. A concertina file divided into months suits some people. The answer is to find the device and system that suit you, ones that are effective, efficient, portable (unless you endlessly want to rewrite your lists), cheap (if you are paying), include work and personal commitments if they are likely to overlap, and above all, that you enjoy using; if you find satisfaction in using the system you will stick with it.

This may seem like a lot of hard, time-consuming work but, like making a budget, the main work only has to be done once. Day-to-day monitoring is a matter of moments, and alterations and improvements are incorporated quickly and easily.

There is one time when this system may cause you more stress—and that is when you think you have lost the diary/notebook/file which has your whole life in it! Have your name and address written *clearly* in the front, state there will be a reward for its return—and be careful!

PROCRASTINATION

Are you already finding reasons why such a system would not work for you, or why it is better to put off starting until the beginning of a new week, a new month, a new year? Why should changes only be made on a Monday? 'Neater' is not an answer.

Procrastination affects most of us at some time. We know what we should be doing but cannot get on with it. For some people it is a deep-seated habit, but it can be broken. Most often we procrastinate when faced with something we do not want to do. One answer is to deal with everything as it crops up, but this can mean that we end up reacting rather than acting, that trivial tasks are given undue importance and we lose sight of priorities. But endlessly putting off doing something can have serious consequences too. Set aside special times for tasks you do not like—then reward yourself afterwards.

Some people like completing unpleasant tasks first thing in the morning; others put them off. Whichever you do, stick to it. If you do not like telephoning, postpone calls to the afternoon on the grounds that it is cheaper then, but do not put them off again until the next day.

If you handle a lot of paper it is easy to let it mount up in piles on your desk. You should aim to handle each piece the absolute minimum of times—once, if possible. One way of checking how often a piece of paper passes through your hands, wasting time on each journey, is to put a dot in a top corner each time you touch it. Do not use a sharp, hard pencil that hardly leaves a mark; choose a solid red felt-tip pen—you want to see each mark. If, by the end of the week, your desk looks as though plague has broken out you know where you have to start.

If you are procrastinating because you cannot make a decision, go back to chapter 8. Decision-making includes what to do, how to do it, what to keep and what to throw out. Some companies—and some people—keep every piece of paper. If you have a lot of space, a good filing system, and someone else to do the filing, fine; otherwise, clutter can be another form of procrastination.

Managing procrastination is the same as managing change; take the first step now, do not expect too much (or try to do too much) too quickly, and do not make excuses for *not* doing something—no exceptions—at least for the first couple of weeks.

Dealing with procrastination also involves knowing when you are doing it. It is easy to fool yourself that activity, any activity, is useful. There are all sorts of fairly mindless, trivial chores that mount up and are part of any job. Doing them when you are tired and cannot concentrate, or when nothing else can be done is sensible; planning the Christmas party in June rather than writing a report is procrastination.

CARRYING A TASK THROUGH

Overcoming procrastination still does not mean that every task will be carried through to the end.

Plan

The use of your daily/weekly plan allows you to see how much time you have and need to carry out each task. Plan for an adequate length of time and don't trust to luck that you can squeeze a job into odd moments.

Concentrate

Do *one* thing at a time. Trying to do several things at once invariably leads to something being forgotten, overlooked, or finished inadequately. Uninterrupted time is what counts. A clear couple of hours when you can mount an all-out attack on a problem is worth two days full of interruptions.

Make sure everyone knows you are not to be interrupted—for *anything* (except, possibly, the building being on fire)—and then *you* stick to this as well as everybody else. If people see you wandering about or you ring them on a different matter, then you lose credibility and this strategy will not work again. Either take your phone off the hook or transfer calls, shut your door and see it stays shut.

If you are in an open-plan office try and find a room which you can borrow for a couple of hours. If all else fails put a 'do not disturb' sign on your desk and when someone approaches ignore them, do not look up, do not speak and if necessary point to the sign. It helps to explain *beforehand* what you are doing and why.

If you are in the sort of job or company which would allow you to stay at home for a morning, then this often works best. You do have to be disciplined enough, however, not to get sidetracked by your spouse, the kids, the dog, household chores and so on.

Take breaks

Paradoxically, taking sufficient breaks improves concentration. Working for too long at a time causes boredom to set in, energy to decrease and physical tension to accumulate. A break of a few minutes, particularly changing your position, is important. Walking around the room, standing for a few minutes, doing a few isometric exercises, simply stretching your limbs all help. If you are going to be working on one task all day, then take a walk at lunch-time.

If you are working on a task which cannot be completed in one go, even a day, and other tasks *have* to intervene, plan them carefully. Doing something completely different is useful in terms of a break. A change is not always as good as a rest, but often has to substitute. Thus, if you are writing a report or working with figures, then attending a meeting or talking to people will interfere less with your primary task than moving on to writing something else or working with figures on another project.

DEALING WITH INTERRUPTIONS

Most interruptions are not emergencies. Emergencies are both important and urgent, and have to be dealt with, but not necessarily by you—we will look at delegation next.

Some unscheduled interruptions are not emergencies, but neither can you refuse them—your boss suddenly wanting to see you, for example—but many interruptions can be managed.

Plan

Make sure that in your weekly plan you have a time when subordinates or even peers know they can come to discuss problems, ideas and issues. Make it clear when you are available and make sure you are. Also explain on what issues people *can* interrupt you and what can be postponed.

Appointments

Unless it is your job to deal with people who 'drop in', use an appointment system. Find out why people want to see you so you can have relevant material to hand.

Appointments can also be used with co-workers, but make sure someone can see you reasonably quickly, that you do not keep people waiting, and that you do not postpone and cancel meetings. Such habits will encourage people to grab you when they can.

Screening

If you have a secretary use him or her to screen telephone calls, visits by others and so forth. Do not be rigid, however, about always knowing what someone wants to see you about first—it may be confidential or personal, and this should be accepted as reason enough.

Learn to say 'no'

Say you cannot stop for a chat now—and mean it. With persistent interrupters keep working and do not meet their eye. Suggest a time when you could meet to talk about the issue. If it is important they will come back; if it is trivial, they will not bother.

Keeping someone standing or standing yourself, means that they are less likely to stay and chat. Where possible set time limits—'I can see you for five minutes. If it will take longer than that, what about 3 p.m.?' If you do this, *stick to it*. Once you allow people to say 'It will only take a couple of minutes' and then run on for half an hour, you have lost control and they will do it again.

Going to someone else's office is often quicker than that person coming to you as you can terminate the meeting more easily. Before you go, however, ask yourself how necessary it is for you to interrupt someone else.

Telephone

A secretary should be screening calls. In an open-plan office where several people share one phone, take it in turns to answer for a set period, taking messages for each other. Either ring back or ask callers to ring back at a specified time—and make sure you do it. If your circumstances warrant it, consider an answering machine.

When people do phone, do not chat; stick to the point. When you phone others, ask if it is convenient to talk, and if not, when it will be. Discourage friends from phoning you for social reasons at work and if necessary, ask your family not to ring you with a list of things to collect on the way home.

DELEGATE

Delegation is basic to time management—sometimes you simply *cannot* do everything yourself—yet it is something many people find difficult to learn.

- It's easier to do it myself
- It's faster to do it myself
- If you want a good job doing, do it yourself
- I haven't got time to show her how to do it
- He couldn't do it
- She never does it the way I would
- At the end of the day, I'm responsible
- I don't trust him to do a good job

. . . and so on. The list of reasons why people do not want to delegate is nearly as long as their list of reasons why they cannot put new ideas into practice today.

Delegation means giving someone a task to do, making sure it is something he or she can do, making that person responsible for it (even if overall or legally, responsibility or accountability is still yours) and, most important, giving them enough authority to enable him to carry out the task without you interfering. Delegation is not passing on boring tasks that neither you nor anyone else wants to do. Neither is it passing on things you personally do not like or find difficult. Some delegated tasks may well be boring but some should be fulfilling, challenging and positive.

It is *not* faster and easier to do everything yourself. If it really were you would not be suffering from the stress which currently assails you. It might well be true that *today* you will have to do something because there is not time to teach someone and still meet a deadline, but next week you can plan an afternoon to teach someone what is involved—can't you? Teaching someone takes time now but it *does* save time in the future.

Imagine if you had never taught your children how to dress themselves—do up buttons and zips, tie shoelaces, comb hair and so on. How much longer would it take you to leave the house in the mornings than it does now?

When delegating a task make sure *you* know what you are asking someone to do, and then make sure *they* know. Meet with them and, unless it is one simple process, make sure they take notes. The areas to be covered should be:

- An introduction and possible background material. This may include why you are giving the task to them
- An outline or overview of the task
- A description of the task, broken down into objectives or goals
- An indication of time scale, performance standards, how these will be measured, and so forth
- An outline of areas of responsibility and authority
- Questions and possible discussion
- Asking your colleague to tell you what they have to do—to check understanding
- Discussing feedback, follow-up and procedures for checking on progress

There is a difference between knowing exactly what it is you want done and how it should be done and allowing someone to make their own decisions and do it their way. The latter is delegation, the former simply carrying out your instructions. If your tendency is towards the former (and you should question whether it really is necessary), then make sure the individual you are giving the task to knows this and knows *exactly* what you want. It is highly frustrating to carry something out and have it returned because you have not done it exactly as someone else wants. If you have already made a certain decision it is often better to do so upfront, than to pretend to a democracy that does not really exist.

Spend time with your secretary or assistant at the beginning of each day (or week, as appropriate) to outline your plans, agree tasks and priorities, and organize yourselves jointly.

Good support staff will only stay with someone who uses them well and who delegates appropriately. If you do not do this they will leave to find someone who will.

WORK ENVIRONMENT

Planning your work environment is also part of time management. It saves time to have things you use a lot within reach, and to have sufficient supplies of materials so that you do not have to stop work to fetch them. Arranging your environment is very much a matter of personal choice. Some people find anything extraneous to the task distracting; others find flowers or a family photograph a pleasant reminder that there is more to life than the present work crisis, or a way of switching off and relaxing for a moment while they contemplate them.

Cluttered or tidy desks are another personal preference. Although many people insist that clearing your desk at night is essential, that you should only have out papers relating to the task in hand, this does not suit everyone. If you are someone for whom 'a messy desk is a sign of a messy mind' or who feels uncomfortable or stressed by an untidy environment, then you should take steps accordingly.

If these things do not bother you, then your working environment will look very different. But you should still have a system—having piles of papers which have to be waded through every time you need to find something because you do not like filing is inefficient, as is believing that if you have papers on your desk, you won't forget about them. Add the task to your list and keep the papers safely until you need them. Urgent papers do not work themselves to the top of a pile— but tasks do move up your list!

Much depends on what you are doing. A variety of small discrete tasks probably means it is better to clear away as you go along. Papers relating to one on-going task can be left out, if it means you can pick up and carry on exactly where you left off the night before. If you are in the fortunate position of having enough space you might be able to give an on-going task a desk to itself, piles of relevant paper and all, and maintain order on your main desk.

Whatever you do, look for what you are comfortable with and what works for you. Avoid becoming so obsessional about tidiness that you spend 80 per cent of your time putting things away, or so messy that you are forever looking for things.

HAVE APPROPRIATE SKILLS

It is a great help in managing your time if you know both what you have to do and how to do it. The next two chapters consider other areas of skill which, as well as reducing stress in themselves, may also help you to manage your time more efficiently.

RESPECT TIME

Respecting your time means using it as you want to, to do the things you want. Resting, relaxing and enjoying leisure activities are not wasting time, but making positive use of it. Feeling restless, bored or frustrated are not good uses of time. You respect your time by managing interruptions better, by planning, by being able to take advantage of opportunities when they arise. If necessary, make appointments with yourself or your family in your diary until you shed the habit of working all the time.

You should also respect other people's time. Needless interruptions when they are busy are inconsiderate. Keeping someone waiting, never being on time for appointments, handing in work to be done at the last minute all show that you have no consideration or respect for the other person. It is likely to indicate that you believe yourself to be more important than they are, that they do not really count. You might see it as a sign of business, importance and power, but others are more likely to interpret it as being inefficient, badly organized or plain rude.

Lastly, remember that doing a job well is not the same as spending a lot of time on it.

10
Communication

Communicating with others can be a source of stress which is often overlooked unless you consider yourself shy or are faced with an unusual major communication task. Nevertheless, the way in which we communicate and interrelate with others can be a vital strand in managing stress. This chapter and the next deal briefly with these issues. If you believe that you have major problems in either of these areas you will probably need to read further on the subject, and I refer you to the suggested further reading list on page 137.

Some jobs rely heavily on communication with others. Salesmen and journalists, doctors and teachers, politicians and clergy all have very different jobs, but all require good communication skills. If communicating is part of your job then relevant aspects will probably have been included in your training. Salesmen need different skills from novelists and will make use of different personal talents as well as a different medium.

For the rest of us, there are a number of areas of communication which are basic to our everyday life and work, and it is these we will consider now.

SOCIAL SKILLS

Social skills are the nuts and bolts of social interaction. They include verbal and non-verbal behaviour and, at their most basic, mean nothing more than acting appropriately in any given situation. The definition of 'appropriate' takes into account both prevailing social and cultural norms as well as what you, and others, want to get out of the situation. Upsetting people, making them angry, sad, anxious or disappointed may be a sign of skilled behaviour if this is what you set out to do, or of unskilled behaviour if you hoped for the opposite effect.

Assertive behaviour

Assertiveness is probably the most written-about and talked-about aspect of social skills but perhaps not everyone is clear what it means. Being assertive involves knowing what your rights are, or what you want out of a situation, and standing up for this, at the same time not infringing on the rights of others. It is largely the last part of the definition which separates assertive behaviour from aggressive behaviour.

Confusion exists in many minds over what exactly assertion is and how to display it. There has been a tendency to describe the way men behave, particularly in work situations, as appropriate, skilled, assertive behaviour. This has led to many women seeking to learn male ways of responding and managing and this tends to go with an acceptance of the status quo and establishment—except, possibly, that it indicates a desire to see more women in positions of power and influence.

Other women see assertiveness as the right to behave as they want—as women—which involves different types of behaviour from men. There is less 'dress for success' and more concern for individuality, less competition and more co-operation, less emphasis on control and thinking and more on expressing and feeling. Such women are likely to be more concerned with changing and improving working relationships and conditions than accepting current rules and learning to play by them. They also want to see more women take their place higher up the corporate or professional ladder.

It is very difficult to both change the rules and still reach the top, especially in traditional professions and occupations. Despite a growing acknowledgement in some circles of the different skills and styles women may bring to management, it is probably wise to know which for you is the greater priority—getting on or changing the way people get on. The need for compromise in various areas then becomes more clear and can be seen as the only way of pursuing these two goals relatively free from internal conflict.

There has been a tendency to neglect men in much of the training work on assertiveness, other than to use them as role models. 'Assertiveness training for men' tends to conjure up unlikely pictures ranging from teaching men how to batter their wives to shouting louder than anyone else in the money markets. This overlooks the central issue that many men do not feel in control of their lives, find themselves doing things they do not want to do, not doing things they want to do, and finding it difficult to express themselves.

Some of the basic problems are the same for men and women, although the specifics will be different. Many people find it difficult to show their feelings, although men tend to find it harder to express positive feelings than negative, and women tend to find expressing negative emotions more difficult. Both may have problems saying 'no', but the reasons behind this will be different (between individuals as well as the sexes).

It usually helps to examine the reasons why you behave as you do, and what unrealistic ideas and expectations stop you doing what you want (see chapter 3).

It is also useful to examine the consequences of your present behaviour to see whether you are really achieving what you want. Often people are non-assertive because they want to be liked, and saying no or making an unpopular decision might make people dislike them. If you agree to do something, however, and then do it badly, conveniently 'forget' to do it, or do it with a lot of sighs, moans and a martyred air, then this is unlikely to go down well. Sometimes by *not* doing what you want you still end up achieving the effects you feared.

Non-assertiveness can also lead to lack of appropriate competition, for example, not seeking promotion or applying for a particular job because you do not believe you could do it (when everyone knows you can). Being under-challenged, which this approach can lead to, can cause as much stress as being pushed too far.

Assertiveness is a state of mind as much as it is having particular verbal and non-verbal communication skills. It is also about having a choice, and exercising that choice. It is being able to say that you do not *choose* to claim your rights in every situation, because you know that if you wanted or needed to, you could.

PERSON PERCEPTION

The first thing to understand when trying to improve communication and social skills is how you perceive others, how you make judgements of them, and the kind of judgement you are prone to make. Even before this, some people need to accept that they *do* make judgements, and on little information.

We use facial and bodily appearance, how people dress, speak, behave, who and what they choose to surround themselves with and every scrap of evidence we can to make deductions about them. This is both natural, reasonable and necessary. We need some cues to help us to know how to act or react with the people we meet.

There is a number of pitfalls, however, which are common to everyone and should be avoided. It is easy, once you have made up your mind about someone, to either reject or simply not see pieces that do not fit your pattern. Ultimately this gives a very biased, one-sided picture if nothing is done to redress the balance. When someone does something you consider 'out of character' ask yourself whether this is really so, or whether your opinion of that person is not limited.

In our search to make sense of other people we often jump to conclusions about them, and then persist in believing these conclusions either without checking them out or in the face of contradictory evidence. This often takes the form of arrogance, assuming you know more about a person than they know themselves. You are given an explanation or reason by someone, but you choose to believe your own, usually negative, version.

This stems, at least in part, from the belief in the workings of a 'dynamic unconscious' (that part of the mind which, although unconscious, still affects our behaviour) and that we can understand someone's 'real motives'. We can be so sure of our ability to read people that we lose sight of how much we are assuming. You may have a suspicion that an employee's timely ill health conceals an inability to do the work or finish it on time, or a trip to a rugby international. But people do fall ill, and at awkward times. If a colleague has a heart attack and you hesitate before ringing for an ambulance, and hear yourself saying 'You are only doing that because you haven't finished the end-of-year report', then maybe it's time to reassess your judgement of people!

We frequently attribute all kinds of characteristics to people on the basis of very flimsy evidence, and then act as though such attributes are proven fact. We make judgements without even realizing it. 'He drives too fast' is a judgement of someone's driving ability; even 'He drives fast' is. The only objective statement would be 'He drove at 60 mph.' But we may go on to make other judgements: this person drives too fast, therefore 'he's aggressive', 'she wants to prove she's as good as a man', 'he's adolescent', 'she's got a death wish.' Problems arise when you respond to someone as though this is fact—*without checking it out further*. And such behaviour can be self-fulfilling. Behave to someone as though you believe he is aggressive and two things are likely: firstly, he will respond as though he *is* aggressive (because that is how you have set the situation up) and secondly, he is likely to take exception to *your* manner—which he will probably see as aggressive!

Even Freud was moved to remark in response to a comment about the hidden meaning of his smoking habits, 'Sometimes a cigar is only a cigar.'

Non-verbal communication

There is a number of books on the market, mainly American, which suggest that it is possible to learn to 'read a person like a book' by understanding what a person's body language 'really means'. By knowing what is unconsciously meant when someone leans back in a chair you then have an advantage over him or her.

Whilst there is some truth in the notion of a language of non-verbal behaviour, it tends to be overstated. The behaviours to which we can reliably attribute meaning are fairly gross—subtleties are more individual. You may learn to read a particular person well, but not be able to apply the same interpretation to another.

Culture plays an important part in non-verbal communication, and behaviours have different meanings. What is considered normal and accepted varies. For example, people from Mediterranean countries gesticulate and touch more than northern Europeans do. People from Arab countries tend to stand closer to each other than the British. It is as well to remember that there are more cultural differences between Britain and America than we often acknowledge, and standards applied or suggested in American books may not be appropriate in Britain—or vice versa.

Learning to read and express appropriate body language often features in all kinds of communication courses, ranging from negotiating to selling, teaching to patient interviewing.

CHAINS OF COMMUNICATION

Much has been written about different chains and patterns of communication and the effect these have. Briefly, all that needs to be mentioned here is to consider whether you are in an 'open' or 'closed' system.

In a 'closed' system there is likely to be a rigid chain of communication, both up and down the hierarchy; breaking out of this is very difficult. Members of such a system feel that they are not free to express what is on their minds, and that independent thought or action cannot be displayed and is actively discouraged. If they do speak out they expect to be ignored at best, most likely criticized or ridiculed, and victimized at worst. In general a negative air of non-co-operation and non-support pervades.

In an 'open' system, however, people feel they have the right to voice their opinions and to speak freely about any issue which is of interest or concern to them. They may know that they will not always have any impact or influence but they also know they can speak without fear of reprisal. People will generally be positive and supportive of one another and a good atmosphere will exist for a free exchange of ideas. Difficult topics will be discussed rather than hidden, releasing tensions which may otherwise fester in a group and lead to low morale and inefficiency.

These are very general areas and it is outside the scope of this book to explore them in detail. If you are aware, however, that your inability to interact well with people contributes to your stress levels then it is well worth exploring these areas further. There is, however, one aspect of communication which is both a cause and a symptom of stress to which we will devote more detailed attention. This is arguing.

DISCUSSING OR FIGHTING

All too often a difference of opinion can lead to both raised voices and raised blood pressure rather than a reasoned exchange of ideas. Although the dictionary defines argument as 'reason advanced for or against a proposition or course', most of us think of an argument as an emotionally charged challenge of another's point of view; someone who is argumentative is considered difficult rather than logical. It is the common assumption that differences of opinion almost inevitably lead to frayed tempers and that they cause people either to seek to avoid an argument, or to launch into one, set to win at all costs and no matter who is hurt in the process—themselves included. The reasoned discussion becomes a slanging match with no holds barred.

In some cases winning at all costs might be more important than maintaining a good relationship with the person with whom you are having the discussion. To call this person 'your opponent' immediately raises the emotional tone.

This brings into focus the meaning of 'winning'. Is 'to win' a reasonable goal? What does it mean? Have you 'won' when someone is grovelling at your feet in agreement, when they walk off in a huff, burst into tears, or never speak to you again? A cheap jibe may give you the last word, but may cause you to lose a friend or the respect of a colleague. Are you seeking to change someone's opinion or do you want them to change their behaviour? It is easy to lose sight of your aim once you become obsessed with point-scoring.

Rules for arguing can be divided into those for 'fighting dirty' and the Marquess of Queensberry rules for 'fair fighting'. In between falls a group of behaviours best described as tactics or, to use Stephen Potter's well-known phrase, ways of getting 'one up'. Some people consider the latter legitimate and others see them as cheating—much depends on whom the argument is with. What may be acceptable to a business rival or even colleague, may not be to your spouse. Fighting fair may take what some see as the 'fun' out of the argument, but that depends on what your objectives are. If all you had to do was point out the logical inconsistencies of the other person's argument there would be no need for rules. Sadly, argument is rarely that simple.

'Fighting dirty'

Below-the-belt tactics in arguing mean anything which provokes defensiveness in the other person and works to prevent change or real communication. Such tactics include:

- **Name-calling** Usually basic, occasionally inventive but rarely witty, calling someone names is one of the fastest ways to lose hold of logic and descend into childishness. It demeans both sides and, when genuinely hurtful, blocks any hope of real communication. Someone who is hurt, angry and defensive is not open to new ideas.
- **Personal criticism** Rather than attacking a person's facts, beliefs or logic you indulge in personal criticism. Instead of simple name-calling you tell the other person that he is bad, useless or wrong. This is done at the expense of either explaining just where their argument breaks down or recognizing your own feelings in the matter. It is easier to say 'you are wrong' than it is 'I'm annoyed with you because . . .'
- **Generalizations** These often accompany personal criticism and the next category, digging up the past. Rather than focusing on a specific issue you say 'you never . . .' or 'you always . . .' Generalizations of this type are accusations rather than facts and can detract from the present issue by allowing the other person to refute the attack with instances of when they did or did not do whatever is in question.
- **Digging up the past** Instead of staying in the here-and-now, you bring up similar instances from the past. In some cases unrelated injustices from weeks, months or even years ago will surface as long-held grudges. Again they divert the argument from its current pre-occupation. It is worth noting, however, that sometimes an issue will be raised which will have to be dealt with, but at another time.

- **Silence**   Although it is very difficult to argue with someone who simply does not answer back, it is also impossible to resolve anything.
- **Non-co-operation**   Not all non-co-operation is as basic as silence. It can take many forms of sabotage, from walking away to apparently agreeing to something and then not implementing it.
- **Alliance**   By talking in the plural rather than in the first person you imply that others agree with you. You should only be doing this if you are in the position of formally negotiating on behalf of a group. If you are informally representing the feelings of a group of workers to the boss then you should outline your remit before you start. If you only drag in others as you start losing ground then you are trying to scrape up an alliance where one does not really exist. It also plays a part in a general 'divide-and-rule' policy where an individual tries to set factions within an office or department against each other. Unless done by a master manipulator it is likely to backfire as people check out with each other what is being said about them and on their behalf.
- **Mind-reading**   Rather than responding to what someone says you respond to what you think they are *really* saying. You often end up talking about two completely different issues. At its most arrogant and foolish it can prevent all communication. You assume you know what the other person will say and therefore do not ask. Thus you never have to deal with conflict or disagreement.

Fighting fairly

- **Talk in the present**   It is only the present you can change, not the past. The past gives us experience from which to learn, not a weapon to batter the other person with.
- **Be specific**   Identify what particular change you want, in terms of what, where, when and how.
- **One change at a time**   This ties in with being specific. Discussing a number of issues or asking for a number of changes at a time causes confusion and frustration.
- **Present your side of the argument**   This involves explaining your thoughts, opinions and feelings and taking responsibility for them, without laying blame on the other person. Blaming and attacking others leads them to become defensive and they may seek to attack you. The argument sinks to critical judgements, generalizations and name-calling.

It also involves speaking for yourself and not trying to create an illusion of more power by using 'we'. You imply the other person must now agree with you.

Taking responsibility for your feelings means saying 'I feel . . . when you . . .' rather than 'you make me . . .' If you are becoming angry that is your responsibility, not something the other person is forcing upon you.

- **Explain what you will do**   State clearly what it is you want, and what you are willing to do to achieve your goals. If you are asking others to do a lot for you, ask or suggest what you might do for them. Trading or exchanging is likely to cause better long-term agreement or change than if all the giving is one-sided.

- **Explain the impact of the other person's behaviour**   This is important if you are asking someone to do *less* of something. The impact may include your feelings as well as practical points—'I feel angry when you give me letters at a quarter to five and I have to work late to finish them. You haven't asked if this is convenient', as well as 'Letters typed after 4.30 miss the post.' Different situations and people call for different amounts of disclosure.

- **Complete interactions**   Walking off in a huff is one way to stop an interaction, but so too can jumping to conclusions about what the other person says and reaching a shaky, premature agreement without checking out exactly what is meant.

These rules should cover most everyday discussions and arguments. Professional negotiators will find them naive no doubt, but their aims as well as rules are different. Tactics which you may or may not want to explore include:

- **Contradictory principles**   Everyone can manage to state (and see) the conflict in an argument when presented as 'I know you said you did not want me to work overtime, but at ten to five you also said it was vital this was finished tonight.' More inventive is to say, when confronted by an accusation of not doing something exactly as specified: 'I know how you deplore people who cover up a lack of original thought/common sense/spotting opportunities by always doing only exactly what they are told.' The aim is to point out that the other person's argument contradicts principles which you know they believe in, and furthermore, they know you know. If you get to the stage of he knows you know he knows you know—and can keep a grip on the logistics of such interactions —then you are just about home and dry.

- **Non-verbal skills**   Speaking loudly, clearly, quickly and fluently are clear signs of assertive behaviour; interrupting and gesturing forcefully may be assertive or aggressive; thumping the table is aggressive; and thumping the other person may result in a charge of assault as well as putting your point across.

More subtle assertive cues to give you the upper hand in an argument include being physically dominant, which means having your head higher than the other person's. Tactics range from lifts in shoes and standing when someone is sitting, to having a low, squashy chair opposite your higher, more formal one. Moving into the other's space, either by going to his office, perching on the edge of his desk, picking up their belongings and moving them, and putting your belongings on their side of the desk, will all make them uneasy.

Just as aggressive but even more subtle is to look disinterested, suppress a yawn, let your eyes wander, show sudden interest in some object on the desk—a photograph or paperweight—or wave to someone across the room.

- **Non-verbal cheating** Rather than coming on tough and aggressive, you appear reasonable, willing to compromise and possibly even passive. You use submissive gestures deliberately, leaning forward with head bowed, keeping eyes lowered, nodding and muttering reassuring noises. When the other person begins to believe you are about to concede you quickly interrupt and take the offensive, in the same soft manner. 'That's the most arrant nonsense I've ever heard', said in the same tone as 'You're absolutely right' will take someone a few seconds to catch up with, giving you time to put your points across. With luck you have been labelled as reasonable because of your previous behaviour and the other person should be more prepared to listen to what you are saying.

- **Blind them with science** If not with actual facts and figures, use jargon and meaningless phrases full of polysyllabic words said with an air of reasonable authority—possibly as though to a child. You should be able to lose people and have your points agreed while they are still trying to work out what you said, let alone answer.

- **Performance is all** Philosophers score points for logic and university debating teams maintain that they do, but everyone else knows that a good show of dominance, self-assertion, humour and good-humour win hands down.

When arguing, it is important to remember that we may be attacking something we do not like in ourselves which we project on to the other person. Even if they *do* have this trait we still may be more annoyed at ourselves than at them. We also fall into the trap of seeing the other person as totally in the wrong. Isolating what is good as well as wrong in the arguments can be helpful, and it is unlikely that someone is totally in the wrong in everything they believe and do. Find out where you agree and build on that. Believing that arguing or having a difference of opinion (however you want to put it) need not be destructive, but can be a healthy way of resolving issues, leading to constructive solutions and/or a release of tensions, is the first step to positive debate.

SPECIFIC COMMUNICATION SKILLS

Promotion brings with it the need to learn and use new communication skills as well as new management skills. Make sure you have both—go on training courses if necessary. The techniques you need to acquire cover everything from writing reports or articles, making presentations, giving papers at conferences, teaching others and giving speeches.

For very special and specific tasks you may consider hiring a professional, perhaps to write an important speech or your curriculum vitae.

11
Relationships at work

Stress can arise from relationships at work on a number of levels. These range from an inability to perform well in a particular role because of misunderstanding over what is required from the role of 'boss' or 'subordinate' or because of lack of skills (particularly management skills) to simply not liking someone with whom you have to work closely.

Sex differences are important to how problems are tackled in many areas of work, and never more so than here. How particular behaviour is described will depend very much on the sex of the person acting that way. We are all aware, or should be, that what is seen as assertive in a man is often seen as aggressive in a woman. Even aggressiveness will be accepted from a man under certain circumstances whereas in a woman it is usually beyond the pale. It also means that acceptable and appropriate behaviour for dealing with some of these problems may depend on whether you are a man or a woman.

CHANGE INVOLVES OTHERS

Managing stress means making changes—in the way you think and feel, in the way you behave, and quite possibly in your environment. Such changes affect not only yourself, but also those with whom you work. Whilst it would be inappropriate to discuss all the changes you have made or intend to make with people at work, some discussion is necessary. Colleagues are not white rats responding to changes in experimental conditions and they deserve some consideration, if only from a practical point of view. They will accept and respond better to your changes if they know why and how they are being made, and that they are not just a whim or a reflection on them.

If, as a way of managing your time better, you decide to meet every morning with your secretary or assistant to explain to them why and what you are hoping to achieve by doing this, and ask for their views, will avoid you causing other people stress as they will worry about what has caused the changes. Many will jump to the conclusion that they have done something wrong and that for some reason you no longer trust them. A stressed, paranoid person is not going to work very efficiently.

ROLES

The word and concept 'role' come to us directly from its theatrical usage; indeed, there are many similarities between playing a role on a stage and playing a role in life. Roles are positions or characters, not people. When we see someone in terms of a 'role', be it boss or subordinate, doctor, secretary, executive or social worker, there are certain actions we expect from that person. A 'role', by definition, prescribes certain actions and, whilst it always contains some aspects which must be performed, some degree of 'creative interpretation' is usually permitted.

Your job description covers the aspects of the role which you must perform—but rarely lays down how to perform them. Some jobs allow more creative interpretation than others. Your environment, your dress and your actions may be highly controlled but your role usually allows some ways in which you can be individual. Judges, for instance, are strictly bound by their role in most areas, but can assert independence and individuality in their sentencing (within limits).

Since all of us fill a number of roles it is inevitable that at times there will be conflict. Role conflict is usually associated with pressure coming from two or more sources at the same time which are incompatible (for whatever reason). It can arise in a variety of ways. Firstly, conflict may arise within a role. You may be given work by more than one person and time demands make it impossible to do it all; one person's instructions do not tie in with another's; or someone deliberately gives you contradictory information.

A second type of conflict will occur when different roles overlap in terms of their demands and expectations. Either you fulfil more than one role at work, or roles from outside the work place intrude on work or vice versa. Personal and family stresses will inevitably interfere with work at times and to assume this will never happen is irrational. The problems of the working mother spring immediately to mind. These are issues which have to be solved by each individual as only he or she can view all the options and determine priorities.

Role conflict of this kind is often tied up with the demands work makes on your time and can sometimes be dealt with by examining your assumptions about the role as well as other peoples'. A woman returning to work after being at home with children will need to reassess how she sees the roles of wife and mother in the light of the additional demands of having a job. Her husband and children will also have to re-examine their expectations and modify their requirements.

Another type of conflict arises when personal beliefs, values or needs are violated by certain duties at work. It may be possible, in some cases, to negotiate changes to your job but if this is not so and you cannot or do not want to change your beliefs and values, in some instances the only option may be to give up the job, because at this point you and it are incompatible.

The cost of these types of role conflict can be great in terms of increased stress and tension, lower job satisfaction, poor job morale, and reduced or lack of confidence in the employer or the organization. Poor relationships at work are also likely to ensue, detracting from your trust, respect and liking for your colleagues.

Role ambiguity can also give rise to stress. Trying to fulfil the demands of a role which is poorly defined can be very draining. Ambiguity can be reflected in a variety of ways: for example, your goals and objectives lack clarity, colleagues' and bosses' expectations are vague or not understood, the job's scope and responsibility are unclear, as are job requirements. Knowledge about the prospects of promotion and what it will be based on might also be lacking. Working conditions such as these will contribute to job stress and tension, lack of job satisfaction, a sense of futility and frustration, and possibly low or reduced self-confidence, lowered morale and poor interpersonal relationships.

Sometimes the problem arises from a job which is poorly defined in the first place but often, where it is coupled with problems of time, a well-defined job becomes cluttered with self-imposed tasks. How to manage this has been covered in chapter 9.

A certain amount of role ambiguity may be expected in many jobs. It only becomes a source of stress when the vague areas outweigh or outnumber the areas which are clear, or when heavy responsibilities or unpleasant tasks are involved.

Responsibility brings us to the last of the role demands related to stress. It will tend to be directed either towards things or to people. Responsibility for people includes their work, and also their development, welfare and safety. Responsibility for things includes not only buildings, equipment and money, but also, implicitly, for people.

(Buildings and equipment have to be safe; without them and without money, people would have no jobs.) Being responsible for people is likely to carry the greatest stress, and that this is an indirect aspect of responsibility for things should always be borne in mind. Air-traffic controllers, for example, belong to a group with very high responsibility in all areas, and show higher rates of stress-related illness than airmen.

In most cases, responsibility assumes a measure of control in terms of decision-making and authority. Where there is responsibility but no authority stress will be greatest.

We will look at three basic working roles and briefly outline areas of potential problems and stress.

Being a boss

The role of 'boss' implies behaviours such as leadership, management and decision-making. The interpretation of the role depends on a number of factors, including individual personality, type of company/ work and organizational dictates. The style of management may be controlled from the top or left open to individual managers. Since the level of morale in a company or department depends more on management practice than on anything else, developing the 'right' style of management is vital.

Although there are many theories of management and corresponding styles, the crucial difference is whether you concentrate on the task or the people. Few managers can get away with being totally task-orientated: managing people is a major part of the job, whether you are a director or a foreman. In some situations, including other members of the department in decision-making may not be possible or appropriate, but they can still be involved in the whole project. Telling someone he does not need to understand why he is doing something, he should just do it will lead to demoralization faster than almost anything else. The armed forces may argue that people need to take orders without question, and in their particular case there may be some truth to this. Likewise in emergencies there is often no time for debate and one person's judgement must be trusted. Nevertheless, people follow orders better if they have faith in the person giving them, and believe he or she knows what he/she is doing and cares about them as people. This will be easier to achieve if you demonstrate at times other than the heat of the moment that you will explain reasons why, that you are competent and that you do not see your workers as machines.

Having a good working relationship with subordinates as well as peers can reduce the stress on a boss fairly dramatically. Managing your time better often contributes to this; you delegate more appropriately and enable others to plan their work better and not be continually rushed. Knowing your own objectives, whether for yourself or a particular task, should mean that the way in which you pass on information, plans, tasks and so forth will be clearer and more easily assimilated.

In addition to this, it is important to demonstrate a genuine concern for others as people, show solidarity in bad times as well as good and be able to release some of the tension at critical moments. Giving feedback to staff is crucial, not only when something is wrong, but also when things go well or someone has performed 'over and above the call of duty'.

Some stresses, such as being held responsible and accountable, also come with being the boss. These are intrinsic to the role and have to be accepted. If you have major problems in these areas then consider whether you have unrealistic expectations of yourself or the situation.

Finally, there is the 'lonely at the top' syndrome. Support is important for everyone, at all levels, and will be discussed in a later section (see page 122).

Being a subordinate

The notion that the people with real stress are high-powered executives is no more than a popular myth and recognizing this is the first step in managing the stress derived from the role of subordinate. High levels of stress are found much more commonly in subordinate occupations. Acknowledging that you are stressed, that many people in your position are stressed and, furthermore, that you have a right to be stressed is the first hurdle.

I have already mentioned that working on a fixed-pace job is more stressful than working on an unpaced job. Machines take no account of human needs, and you need not be working on a factory assembly line to feel as though you are.

Bosses who work to their own pace with no thought of how long it will take you to do something are a common complaint. Pointing out that a 10-page report cannot be typed in half an hour may or may not be successful. If most of your stress derives from your boss's way of working you have several options. One is to say there is nothing you can do and suffer; another is to change bosses; or, more constructively, you may try to confront him or her with the problem. It helps to have details (as ammunition) and plans (to wave aside objections that 'nothing can be done'). When I discussed time management I suggested you keep a diary—this comes in useful here for demonstrating both *what* you do and *how long* it takes.

Putting all the blame on the boss is unlikely to create the right atmosphere for change, and assertiveness principles may have to be compromised slightly. Priorities need establishing, and not just in terms of what projects are important; is sorting out business to take precedence over ordering flowers for a forgotten anniversary? And is working overtime every night this week and having a day off in lieu next week the best way to deploy your time? Make it clear where the loss of productivity will occur, in work terms, if you move on to a new task. Rather than saying 'I'll miss my lunch', assume you will still have lunch and say 'X will not be done.'

Creative interpretation of some subordinate roles seems to include the need to cope with every demand, no matter how outrageous. Individuals can end up blaming themselves for their inability to be in more than one place at a time, or type letters, photocopy a report and make phone calls all at once. If you find yourself in this position you need to examine the irrational ideas which make you demand so much of yourself.

It may be difficult to overcome the years of conditioning which say you have no control, that you have to do as you are told with no questions, but learning to see where you *can* exercise choice and seeing how you may be perpetuating the situation are crucial. If you always manage to do things against the odds you are teaching your boss that he need not improve your conditions of work, rather than appearing a miracle-worker. Your credibility is soon lost if you keep saying 'it cannot be done' and then do it.

The subordinate role means that you take direction from others; it does not imply that you have to do so like a mindless robot. If you emphasize work productivity and goals, a reasonable boss will discuss an issue with you. An unreasonable boss will ignore everything except their own wishes and demands. Whether you seek a transfer or not depends on the job market and availability of change, your need to earn, and your sense of self-preservation. Feeling guilty about leaving, saying that 'no one else would put up with him', and so on, stems from your need to be needed, fear of change, belief that you do not deserve better or a range of other irrational ideas. Make decisions in terms of yourself and your health—emotional and physical.

Being a team member

Being a member of a team does not mean that you are all equal—

ranks and roles still exist. If you do not understand this then conflict with other team members will result. The popular wisdom is that men make better team members than women because they usually have a stronger history of playing team sports. They know, supposedly, that there is a captain, that everyone has their position and that this position governs their moves, strategies or behaviour. Women, so they say, because of their lesser experience of such sports, have little sense of hierarchy, rank or position. Rather than sticking solely to their 'position' or job, they run around doing all kinds of extra things, tasks that someone else has left undone or for which no one is really responsible. This, the suggestion goes, confuses the other team players as they cannot count on the person to be where they expect her to be.

Whilst this may hold true of some departments or teams it is unlikely that all operate like this. What is certain is that it is important to understand how your team functions, whether roles are rigidly adhered to or if there is room for flexibility, and within what limits. Being a team member means doing what you are supposed to, when and how you are supposed to. It means informing others about tasks left undone, not assuming that you can go ahead without doing them. What may seem helpful behaviour to you can be construed as interference by others. Working as part of a team means co-operating with, not competing against, others. It means understanding individual roles and the team's interpretations of them, not experimenting with an individualistic interpretation. Credit belongs to the team for a job well done, and should not be appropriated by one person. If you are strongly Type A (see pages 45-57), very competitive or highly individualistic, then you are likely to see being a member of a team restrictive. Deciding where you *must* conform and where you are freer to please yourself is dependent on the situation and the other players.

SOCIAL SUPPORT AT WORK

Sadly, more is written about office politics and getting ahead in the competition stakes than is written about positive relationships at work. Other people may be a source of stress, but they can also be a source of support, comfort and satisfaction. A good working relationship with colleagues can both reduce stress and provide a source of support in the management of it.

Some occupations seem to go out of their way to discourage mutual aid and succour. Ironically, these are often high-stress jobs, such as the police, where a macho image and 'stiff upper lip' are prized. There is no occupation or organization where only one person is stressed. To assume you are the only person to be worried smacks of an irrational mixture of foolishness and arrogance. As stress-related illnesses and problems lead to an increasing number of lost man-hours the need to deal with the issue is gradually being faced.

Support from an individual or group of colleagues can come in many guises, ranging from a shoulder to cry on to positive help and advice. Constant moaning with no attempt to change matters has no effect in the long run and merely induces a general sense of pessimism, helplessness and hopelessness; being able to share feelings with those in the same position, however, and knowing that you are not alone is an important release and source of support. In some instances a friend at work can offer more support than your family simply because they are in the same situation and understand what you are saying in a way an outsider never could. Sometimes it is difficult for those not in the same situation to accept all you say and to have them question your account only adds to your stress. Colleagues will both be able to accept what you say more readily and, in some cases, point out things you have overlooked.

They can also prove a useful sounding board to try out new ideas for coping and can even provide new strategies themselves. One or two might even serve as role models, even though you may have little interaction with them. Although, in some circumstances, colleagues may help out with stressful work this is usually only a short-term solution to a particular crisis. Trading tasks, however, can sometimes be mutually satisfying.

The most important aspect of social support at work is that it should provide a sense of belonging. Whilst this can include shared responsibility and a sense of involvement, it centres on a solidarity which prevents you feeling isolated or alienated.

It is commonly accepted that women find it easier to develop relationships and are more dependent on them than men. If this is true it means that women are better placed than men to make good use of a social support network. A disadvantage is that women may expect all colleagues to be friends and will try to treat them as such. This is not always appropriate and, since we rarely choose our work colleagues, it is unrealistic to expect them all to be people you would want as friends. This should not mean, however, that your working relationships are difficult. Learning to maintain a good, civil pattern of interaction with everyone at work will reduce much interpersonal conflict and resultant stress.

Those of you who have a strong Type A personality may dismiss the need for social support, tending to stand aloof from others or engaging in competitive rather than co-operative behaviour. You are more likely to see others as a convenient source of blame when things do not go entirely to plan. Your concentration on self will tend to mean that you neither notice nor care what effect this attitude has on those with whom you work. It can also mean that in times of real crisis you end up totally isolated. In less dramatic vein, you might find that some people do not work well with you, either actively or passively withholding their co-operation, and this may ultimately lead to your exclusion from certain sources of information or resources, or general inefficiency regarding your work on the part of others. Most people will not do favours for someone who treats them like a machine— often a faulty machine, at that.

An area which frequently causes problems is when one of two colleagues or friends is promoted. Conflict arises because of the expectations and prescriptions of overlapping roles. The most successful way of dealing with this is to match role to situation, so that at work 'boss' predominates whilst elsewhere 'friend' predominates. It is unrealistic to expect that this will have no impact on your relationship. If you are promoted away from the other person the impact need be minimal, but if you become their supervisor changes will almost certainly occur. However you choose to handle this, being consistent is important. Stress will be exacerbated for both sides if you keep shifting at work from the friendly responses of an equal to being authoritarian or disciplinarian and back again. Neither of you will be sure how you are going to respond to anything and you will start to avoid one another.

12
Person-job fit

Forcing a square peg into a round hole is not a very useful exercise—unless you are in the business of producing dowels! Having the right person in the right job is the dream not only of personnel managers, but of employees as well. Believing yourself to be in the wrong job can be soul-destroying. Although some researchers produce lists of the most stressful jobs, this is not necessarily helpful to the individual. Even if we acknowledge that, for example, being a miner or air-traffic controller is intrinsically more stressful than being a secretary or a statistician, this does not mean that there are no secretaries and statisticians under more stress than some miners or air controllers.

Person-job fit involves two important elements. The first of these is how far the individual's abilities, skills and talents are matched by the demands and requirements of the job, including the job environment. Secondly, fit relates to how far the individual's needs, values and wish to use particular skills and talents are met, or maintained, by the job.

The subject of person-job fit raises a number of wider issues than simply the effect on an individual. Can the work place provide enough square holes for square pegs, or society round pegs for round holes? Should we even expect perfect person-job fit? If so, does this imply a person can only be seen in terms of his job? If we have square people and round jobs which should be modified? Which is easier to modify? How?

Many of the problems people have with their jobs have been discussed in earlier chapters, in terms of the type of demand made on them, the environment, their personality and so forth. Here we look at ways of trying to cope with poor person-job fit.

POOR PERSON-JOB FIT

Staying with the square-peg person and the round-hole job, we can represent the problems diagramatically. Fig 5 shows the most common problem in terms of poor person—job fit, namely that of overwork or inability to meet the demands of the job. The job takes everything the person has and still demands more—whether this be time, energy, talents or skills the person does not possess. People in this situation are likely to suffer from severe time-demand problems, the stress and insecurity of knowing that they are not fulfilling all the functions of their job, and are probably under pressure from both superiors and subordinates to perform better. To this might well be added demands from family or friends who feel they are being ignored as the individual focuses his whole attention on the job.

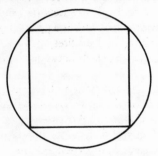

Fig. 5 Over-stretched

People promoted beyond their ability will find themselves in this position, as will those for whom promotion brings tasks for which they have not been trained. Very often such tasks will be managerial and administrative ones. It may be that the individual is in this position not because they have changed job, but because the job has changed around them. The introduction of new technology requires learning new skills. The current economic climate may mean that there have been job losses within the company and people now find themselves having to take on the duties of people who have left and not been replaced. This may simply mean more to do and logistical problems, or may require new skills.

The opposite problem is experienced by those trapped in the situation shown in Fig 6. Here stress stems from under-stimulation; there are no challenges in the job and the individual is frustrated by not being able to use all his skills. The focus for this frustration will vary according to the reason such skills are not valued. Changes in technology may

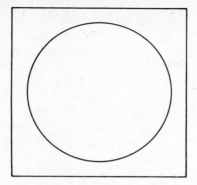

Fig 6   Under-stretched

mean that once-valued skills are now redundant; the worker is likely to vent his resentment on both the new technology itself and those responsible for its introduction. This is a problem with a long historical tradition reaching back to the Luddites, and in recent British history it has been highlighted by the clash between the print workers' unions and Rupert Murdoch.

The resentment can be more personal, however: for example, in the case of a secretary whose hard-won skills in shorthand lie unused because her boss does not like dictating. Anyone who will not delegate may find themselves the focus of feelings or ill will if they prevent those under them using or developing their talents.

Increasing numbers of people find themselves in jobs for which they are over-qualified because of the current high levels of unemployment. In such cases the individual's frustration may be turned outward and directed towards society or the government which has allowed this to happen. Other people will turn these feelings inward and blame themselves for not being able to find a better job. The expression of such feelings will range from demonstrations of self-pity to profound depression requiring medical intervention.

Lastly, some jobs require nothing of the person doing them. This is the assembly-line type of work which could as easily be done by machine or robot. In all these cases the boredom and frustration engendered by the job may well spill over into other areas of life until doing anything that presents a challenge becomes too much trouble.

Most people, hopefully, do not find themselves in either of these last two extreme positions, but in a situation resembling Fig 7. We are able to cope with most of our job to our own and others' satisfaction, with only a few areas where we either do not perform as well as we

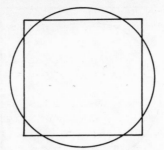

Fig 7   'Normal' work situation

would like, or where we do not have the appropriate skills. Our job fulfills most of our need to express particular talents or parts of ourselves yet still leaves us with enough energy to use those parts of ourselves which the job does not touch or require.

Is there such a thing as a perfect person-job fit? And what does it mean? A round person in a round hole suits a job, can function in it well, has the abilities to carry out the job tasks, and does not feel frustrated by not using abilities which he or she values. The emphasis is on the person fitting the job (see Fig 8). Another variation would be to take the square person and shape the job to fit his needs and talents, with much the same result (see Fig 9).

Most people do not feel the need for job-person fit to be so close. We expect to have not only leisure time, but the energy and drive to use it in ways we enjoy. Very often this means being creative or sporting, or doing something which our job does not offer. Clearly a job cannot fulfil our needs regarding family and friends, but it should give us the time to involve ourselves with them. Although this goes without saying

Fig 8   The 'perfect fit' dream: Fig 9   The 'perfect fit' dream:
the person fits the job   the job fits the person

for most people, some believe that all their time and energy *should* be devoted to their job. And some bosses and companies seem to believe this as well. They are producing people with narrow interests who on retirement or, even worse, redundancy, have nothing left in their life. They have become one with their job and there is nothing else to them.

Measurement of person-job fit can be used both by the organization and the individual. Once someone has been identified as being at risk then various measures can be employed by organizations to deal with this. Such strategies range from special training programmes, in particular skills and stress management courses, to job rotation schemes and job enlargement or enrichment programmes. In extreme cases it may even be necessary to find a more suitable job for an individual. On the whole it would seem that good person-job fit is achieved more easily on an individual basis than at group level and this may well persuade people to take the second course of action.

This would make the individual responsible for his own job-person fit. If someone is to be able to do this successfully, however, the organization must be flexible enough to allow individuals to modify their job demands. Since overall organizational goals and structures will remain this may only be achievable by involving worker organizations and establishing or maintaining good union-management relations.

IMPROVING PERSON-JOB FIT

As mentioned above, improving person-job fit can be the responsibility of either the organization or the individual. To discuss organizational strategies such as selection and training is outside the scope of this book. There are, however, things that you as an individual can learn from organizational strategies, so these elements will be considered.

Selection

Good selection procedures increase the probability of achieving satisfactory person-job fit. This applies not only to the work of the personnel department, but also to delegating tasks or selecting people to work on particular projects within a department. The first step involves a comprehensive analysis of the job in question; it is useful to do this for your own situation if you are experiencing stress.

A job analysis is more than listing the straightforward tasks to be carried out, and should also include what skills and personal qualities are required. Difficult and distasteful aspects of the job should not be overlooked.

In selecting someone for a particular job or task it should be borne in mind that there is usually a number of ways of achieving the same end satisfactorily. Being diplomatic, efficient, putting on a good presentation, having a good bedside manner can all come in a variety of guises. A common mistake is to assume that whoever does the job must do it like you, or as you think they should.

Analyse your own job, in terms of not just the tasks, but also the qualities you think are important as well, whether it is displaying patience or the ability to make snap decisions.

Training

Training comes in two major forms: training *for* a job, and training *in* a job. Having done the former does not necessarily stop you from needing the latter. Training for a job is separate from the work process itself and attempts to fit individuals for a particular career. The availability of and necessity for such training vary with the occupation, but examples include everything from an M.B.Ch.B. (doctor's qualifications), LL.B. (Batchelor of Laws) or M.B.A. (Master of Business Administration) to certificates in shorthand and typing.

On-the-job training is usually less well thought out and less well thought of, and is frequently a mixture of learning skills, learning how your own particular organization works and learning how to fit in. Recognized apprentices may follow well worked-out schemes including day-release courses. Higher up the occupational ladder, the situation is likely to be more haphazard and less suited to either the individual's or the job's needs. You may be sent on a course because the company always sends someone rather than because you or your job require it.

Developing your own training scheme

First look at the tasks your job involves and then decide whether you have all the skills to meet them. Look ahead as you assess your situation so that you consider not just whether, for example, you currently understand and use the new technology, but whether you understand enough to plan ahead with it and develop new applications within your department or company. Other areas to consider include writing reports, public speaking, making presentations, administrative duties, chairing meetings, leading a team and so forth.

Having done this, mull over whether you lack any qualities or skills on a broader level. Differentiate between specific management skills and a more general ability to manage people. Broader qualities include the facility to manage your time, stay on top of things and be assertive.

Making this distinction is not so arbitrary as it may look. In the first group you should have primarily a list of skills which you need because of changes in your job, either through promotion or new work practices and technology. These are skills which you can legitimately expect your company to assist you in obtaining (not, of course, if you said you could do something to get the job!). No one would introduce new machinery on to the factory floor without teaching the operators how to use it, and the same should be true for all levels and types of skill. Ask to go on courses or, if there are a number of you in the same position, bring in a specialist which may cost the company less. This also has the advantage that the course can be tailor-made to the company's requirements.

The second, broader category deals with deficits that you may well not want to reveal and feel that you have to learn to manage on your own. Although some more enlightened companies may send the executives on stress management or time management courses, or even stretch to encouraging women managers to attend assertiveness courses, they are in the minority. Many people believe that to reveal at work that they are under any sort of pressure would be highly detrimental to their career. Sadly, this is more frequently true that it should be. Rather than simply pretending the problem does not exist and hoping it will go away, it is better to face up to the issues involved and do something about it.

Although a great deal can be learnt about stress management from a book—if it is put into practice—some aspects, such as learning to relax, may be more easily developed on a course. Acquiring assertiveness skills can be difficult to achieve in the right balance without some input from others. Courses vary from fairly cheap ones run by local authorities and university extra-mural departments to much more expensive ones run by commercial concerns. Before going on a course find out exactly what it offers and what you get for your money. A higher fee does not necessarily mean a better course; it may just be that you are paying for good hotel accommodation. You may find all you need in a much cheaper local evening class. Professional organizations or other groups often run courses for their members and these may be worth investigating, or even suggesting that they run them in the first place.

A great deal, however, can be accomplished on your own.

Work overload

Most of this book is devoted to the problem of demand outstripping resources. If you are in the situation shown in Fig 5 (see page 126) the areas you should be concentrating on include, in summary:

- **Reducing demand** by (a) considering your irrational and unrealistic ideas about yourself and your job; (b) redefining your job. This includes delegating tasks and making better use of support staff, or giving up old tasks as you take on new ones.
- **Managing time** better (see chapter 9).
- **Improving your skills** and thus taking less time to complete tasks or doing them more efficiently.
- **Changing your job**—or at least considering the possibility. Less money in the short term (or even long term) may be bearable if you enjoy life more, can spend more time with your family or doing other things you enjoy, or find work which lets you use your skills in a way which suits you better. Although expensive, companies which offer career guidance, analyse your abilities, interests and potential, and suggest new possibilities can be very useful. In large companies which encourage internal movement personnel officers may serve the same function.

Work underload

This has been described in less detail but managing the problems shown in Fig 6 (see page 127) includes, in summary:

- **Developing your job** Empire-builders do not recognize job descriptions any more than they recognize territorial boundaries. Look for ways of adding to what you do. This can range from analysing and writing up ideas on data you have been asked to find, to coming up with suggestions for new ways of doing things. Always make sure you have a fully worked-out plan and can argue the case, as it will be more difficult to turn someone down if you do not fall at the first hurdle. You may be privy to information from a lot of different departments. Do something with it; write reports to keep people informed. Mainly you are seeking gaps which you can plug or long-winded, time-consuming channels which you can short-cut. Only take on or develop new work that is going to be of use to you in terms of job development, personal interest or that gets you noticed by the right people. Do *not* wash up the coffee cups because everyone else is too lazy. Sort out other people's messes, by all means, but only if you think you will eventually be able to incorporate the results into your job and be able to take the credit.

- **Use your skills elsewhere** If you are in a job which is beyond developing, or you do not want to develop it because it is essentially not the job you want to do, or even if it is a job you like but it does not require all your abilities, then the option of making use of your skills elsewhere is obvious. It is, however, not always that easy. If you want to do something creative—paint or sing, write or act—there are many obvious outlets, from working on your own to evening classes, amateur dramatic societies and the like. If you feel you want to do something useful or worth while then the voluntary organizations which would welcome you are legion. Almost any skill will be met with delight, from accounting to addressing envelopes. As anywhere else, good managers are often thin on the ground and organizing ability or being able to pull a few strings are useful.

    The major difficulty in putting your skills to work elsewhere is the inertia which stems from being bored all day. Doing nothing much, either physically or intellectually, is not conducive to doing things in the evening or at weekends. The only real way out of this is to force yourself to do something, even if you do not feel like it. As long as you enjoy it, the element of forcing yourself soon disappears.

- **Change your job** You may be trapped in a boring job because of a good salary, or even just a salary. As in work overload, consider whether a reduction in pay would not be compensated in a job you would enjoy more, or by going on a course to learn something new or pursue the qualifications to do what you really want.

ETHICAL ISSUES AT WORK

This is very much an individual problem which it is up to the individual to solve. If you are using the same frame of reference to judge practices at work as you would use to judge practices involving family and friends, with whom human needs come first, then you will often find yourself in a position of conflict. For most businesses money is the bottom line, along with power and growth. Whether you choose to shift your frame of reference is up to you. If you do not then you may be happier working in a different sort of company, or you may choose to make your value system known and seek to alter the fundamental frames of reference.

Agreeing to do something you consider immoral is likely to cause you a great stress; agreeing to do something you know is illegal is just stupid.

13
Preventing
stress at work

Here is a summary of the major themes of this book in terms of preventing stress, as well as managing it, through what the individual, the organization and society can do.

THE INDIVIDUAL

- Ensure good person-job fit or make necessary adjustments
- Develop sensible, rational beliefs and attitudes to yourself, your performance and your job
- Change your behaviour in line with your new attitudes, including reviewing priorities
- Develop the right skills and behaviours to enable you to do your job to the best of your ability
- Develop a good social support network, both at work and with family and friends
- Keep as physically healthy as you can through sensible diet, sleep, exercise and so forth
- Learn to relax
- Learn to use leisure time sensibly

THE ORGANIZATION

- Redesign jobs where necessary to eliminate unnecessary stress
- Provide a sense of involvement
- Provide better training for jobs, especially for promotions
- Provide advice on problems (work and/or personal) and support

from a team of welfare, health and counselling staff
- Make transfers within the company or a move to alternative non-stressful work possible
- Provide support for responsible jobs, and adequate resources and back-up for all jobs
- Provide stress management courses

SOCIETY

- Abandon the myth of the 'stiff upper lip' and encourage a greater sharing of feelings and support
- Abandon the 'glamorous' image of stress in some occupations—long hours, heavy drinking, constant inter-continental travel, tight deadlines and so forth
- Move from prizing competition to encouraging co-operation
- Believe that stress can kill and be willing to do something about it

Further reading

Consumers Association, *Living with Stress* (London: Consumers Association, 1982)

A. Dickson, *A Woman in Your Own Right* (London: Quartet Books, 1982)

M. Gelb, *Body Learning* (London: Aurum Press, 1983)

N. Josefowitz, *Paths to Power* (London: Columbus Books, 1980)

J. LaRouche, *Strategies for Women at Work* (London: Unwin Paperbacks, 1984)

I. Robertson, N. Heather *Let's Drink to Your Health! A self-help guide to drinking* (Leicester: British Psychological Society, 1986)

Video Arts, *So You Think You Can Manage?* (London: Methuen, 1984)

Useful addresses

Please remember to enclose a stamped addressed envelope when writing.

Action on Smoking and Health (ASH)
5-11 Mortimer Street
London W1N 7RH
Pamphlets and lists of local authority smoking clinics

Alcohol Concern
3 Grosvenor Crescent
London SW1X 7EE
List of available services, promotes services and can refer people for
counselling

Alcoholics Anonymous
Local address in telephone directory or
P.O. Box 514
11 Redcliffe Gardens
London SW10 9BQ
Large number of groups throughout Britain holding regular meetings

The British Association for Counselling
37a Sheep Street
Rugby CV21 3BX
Will put you in touch with counsellors in your area

Health Education Offices
Your local office will be listed in the telephone directory and should
be able to give you information on local classes, pamphlets and so forth

Industrial Health Service
Nuffield House
College Road

Rochdale
Greater Manchester OL12 6AE
Will give support and advice

The Industrial Society
Peter Runge House
3 Carlton House Terrace
London SW1Y 5DG
Gives information and runs courses on various skills

Society of Occupational Medicine
Royal College of Physicians
11 St Andrew's Place,
Camden
London NW1
Information and advice

Society of Teachers of Alexander Technique
W. London House
266 Fulham Road
London SW6
Will put you in touch with local teachers

Transcendental Meditation
Roydon Hall
East Peckham
Nr Tonbridge
Kent TN12 5HN
Will give details of courses in your area

TRANX (National Tranquillizer Advisory Council)
17 Peel Road
Wealdstone
Harrow
Middlesex HA3 7QX
Offers advice, information, counselling and groups for those with a
dependence on minor tranquillizers and sleeping pills

Yoga for Health Foundation
Ickwell Bury
Nr Biggleswade
Bedfordshire
Will give details of local and national centres and clubs

Local authority and university adult education evening classes
There will be a wide variety of classes available, some of which might
help you learn new skills such as computing, and also yoga, relaxation
and so forth. Check local information during the summer to enrol
in the autumn

Australia

Healthy Lifestyle
P.O. Box 450
Crows Nest, NSW, 2065
Pamphlets and tapes, courses in stress management

National Heart Foundation of Australia
Located in all Capital Cities
Information available

Alcohol & Drug Information Service
St. Vincents Hospital
Darlinghurst, NSW, 2010
24 hour telephone counselling, assessments and referrals service.
Country Callers: Toll Free (008) 42-2599

Health Lifestyle Courses
Royal North Shore Hospital
St. Leonards, NSW, 2065
Relaxation and stress management courses

Alcoholics Anonymous
Locked Bag No. 4
Beaconsfield, NSW, 2014
Pamphlets, books, regular meetings

Index

goal-setting, 85-6
ineffective ways, 71-5
    alcohol, 72
    drugs, 72-3
    overwork, 74-5
    smoking, 71-2
managing time, see managing time
staying healthy
    exercise, 76-7
    play, 82
    sleep, 77-8
    spiritual beliefs, 81-2
    see also relaxation
see also problem-solving skills
coronary heart disease, 29, 42, 73
Crosland, Anthony, 65

deadlines, 23, 43, 48
decision making, 67
delegation, 94, 101-2, 120
demands, 60, 93, 94, 117
depression, 20-1, 127
    breast cancer and, 36
diet, 18, 53, 73-4
discussing, see communication
divorce, 36
driving, 65-6
drugs, 43, 72-3
dynamic unconscious, 108

early warning signals, 23
eating, 18, 53, 73-4
egoism, 49-50
Ellis, Albert, 37
environmental stress, 40-1, 60-3
euphoria, 27
exercise, 53, 76-7
exhaustion, 28
expectations, 37, 117

fed-up, 23
feedback, 89
fight response, 26-8
fighting, see communication
fitness, see exercise
flight response, 26-8
forward planning, 95-7
frustration, 126-7
    see also boredom

gender differences, 43-4
    in support needs, 123
General Adaptation Syndrome, 26-8
    alarm reaction, 26-8
    exhaustion, 28
    resistance, 28
glamour, 42-3
goal-setting, 85-6

hard-driving style, 18-19
hassles, 37
headaches, 27
health
    General Adaptation Syndrome, 26-8
    physical signs of stress, 29-31
    physiology of stress, 26-9
    stress and illness, 29-31
    see also coping, staying healthy
heart disease, see coronary heart disease
helplessness, 20, 123
hopelessness, 20, 123
hormones, anxiety, 27
hypertension, 29

ideas, see beliefs
incentive, see motivation
indigestion, 29
interruptions, 99-101
irritable bowel syndrome, 29

jet lag, 64-5
job changes, 36
job descriptions, 93-4, 117

laughter, 82
leisure time, 128-9
life events, 35-6
lifestyle, 35-44
    beliefs and attitudes, 37-9
    daily events, 36-7
    environmental stressors, 40-1
    gender differences, 43-4
    life events, 35-6
    meaning in life, 40
    personality type, see personality
    stress as glamour, 42-3
    stress as motivation, 41-3
    support, 39-40
lighting, 62